The Prodigal Son's Father

Tales of a very different sort of Kingdom

Copyright © 2018, Bruce McKibben. All rights reserved.

Cover artwork by Ingrid McKibben Lofnes

This book may not be copied or reprinted for commercial gain or profit. The use of short quotations or occasional page copying for personal or group study is permitted. Permission will be granted on request.

All scripture quotations, unless otherwise indicated, are taken from the Holy Bible, New International Version®, NIV®. Copyright ©1973, 1978, 1984, 2011 by Biblica, Inc.™ Used by permission of Zondervan. All rights reserved worldwide. www.zondervan.com The "NIV" and "New International Version" are trademarks registered in the United States Patent and Trademark Office by Biblica, Inc.™

Scriptures marked The Message taken from The Message. Copyright © 1993, 1994, 1995, 1996, 2000, 2001, 2002. Used by permission of NavPress Publishing Group.

Scripture quotations marked Amplified taken from the Amplified® Bible, Copyright © 1954, 1958, 1962, 1964, 1965, 1987 by The Lockman Foundation. Used by permission. (www.Lockman.org)

Table of contents

Introduction	1
The Kingdom of Heaven is like...	6
The King	12
A Place to Belong	13
The Prodigal Son's Father	26
Extravagant	63
Unshakable	80
The Kingdom	95
To Lose Is to Win	96
Identity	113
Grace and Works	121
A Culture of Freedom	130
The One Thing	149
The Business of Doing Church	161
The Kingdom	197
The Business of the Kingdom	207
The Bride	**240**
Anticipation	241
Transition	248
The Wedding	260
Making Herself Ready	274
Index of Parables	**289**
Acknowledgments	**290**
About the author	**292**

Introduction

Uncommonly normal

You may not have thought much about it, but *normal* is not the same as *common*. Even though most of the people in a culture have a common understanding of something, that understanding is not necessarily normal. The word normal comes from a Latin word referring to something which has been made in accordance with a carpenter's square. So, in a sense, being normal means being in line with the original design.

A huge problem facing us today is that a lot of common understanding is not in line with the perspective of the original designer of this world. God the Creator designed this world to be a place where he and the people he created could enjoy fellowship together. But things aren't much like that today. And now, a lot of what is *normal* seems to us to be backwards, upside down or inside out.

I find this especially true when I read the stories (parables) that Jesus told about how the Kingdom of Heaven works. The more I look at these stories, the more I see that they describe a normal which is quite uncommon. It is a very different sort of Kingdom.

And so, my desire is to learn to see with a *normal* perspective. And, as my vision is being restored, I am learning to walk in accordance with what I see. This book is a result of my initial steps on a journey toward becoming uncommonly normal.

We'll begin with a quick look at why Jesus told stories about the Kingdom.

Next, we'll take a good look at the nature of the King, and how you might need to change the way you think in order to see him more clearly. He is a good King. A very good King. In fact, you might just be surprised by finding him to be very different from what you thought he was like.

From there we'll move on to the culture of the Kingdom. Jesus told a number of parables that illustrate Kingdom values which may be quite foreign to us. But living abundantly in a kingdom means learning to thrive in the culture of that kingdom.

Finally we'll take a look at what the Kingdom longs for: a bride who has made herself ready – a bride who is normal. My prayer is that you will be challenged and equipped to be uncommonly normal in the midst of the common abnormality that surrounds us.

Interpretation

I believe that the Bible is the inspired word of God, and that it is completely true and right. At the same time, the Bible is a composite of many different types of communication. There are clear biblical truths, but there are also historical transcripts, prophecies, illustrations and symbolism; all of which are subject to interpretation. For example, the bible clearly tells us that Jesus will return to this Earth. However, I do not believe that the Bible clearly tells us when, where or how Jesus will return. There are many passages that touch on these questions, but they speak indirectly through imagery, allusion or symbolism and must therefore be interpreted.

An interpretation can be a good thing, but it can also be a little (or even a lot) wrong. To make things even more complex, it is not unusual for a passage to have more than one valid interpretation. A Western mode of thinking has a problem with that – we often tend to think that if one interpretation is correct, then all other interpretations are excluded. But the Bible was written in a Middle-Eastern context, and in that context (I have been told) it is not necessarily a problem for seemingly conflicting interpretations to stand side by side.

Parables are intentionally illustrative. They do not speak biblical truths directly, but illustrate them with symbolism and parallels that must be interpreted in order to extract the biblical truths. So this book could well contain interpretations that might be different from those with which you are accustomed. Keep in mind that one valid interpretation does not necessarily invalidate other interpretations. But, above all, remember that an interpretation is just that: An interpretation. An interpretation will always be colored by the culture and experience of the interpreter. We need to always be open to the leading of the Holy Spirit, who will increase and refine our insight as we walk together with Him in friendship.

I should also mention that I sometimes use terms, such as sonship, which are not gender neutral. When I write about being a son, I am not in any way meaning to exclude women. By son, I mean son or daughter. But consistently using gender-neutral language can be awkward and make for cumbersome writing. Therefore, I have chosen to retain the gender terminology of the parable at hand. For example, the prodigal son's father had two sons. So I refer to sons and to sonship. But the application of the insights here is gender-neutral: we are all, male and female, invited to be sons and daughters of God and to have a son/daughter relationship with him.

Food for thought

As we shall see later, one of the core values of the Kingdom of Heaven is freedom. The freedom to choose wisely can only exist where there is also freedom to act foolishly.

For this reason, I will not endeavor to tell you what to do with the insights you may gain from reading this book. This is not a book about what you must do to be a good citizen of the Kingdom. It is rather an attempt at helping us to think and live more from the perspective of Kingdom culture.

If your view of the Kingdom is primarily colored by following somebody's instructions then you will miss out on much of what is really happening there. Also, if I tell you what to do, then you may choose to reject what I say and never actually face the realities of the Kingdom. Finally, you may not agree with everything I have written, but hopefully you will hold on to the good stuff[1] and at least ponder the weird stuff and the stuff you might not like.[2] The Bible is a multi-dimensional book,

---

1   1 Thessalonians 5:21
2   I welcome your comments about things you may find disagreeable, unpleasant or just plain wrong. And it would please me greatly if you write to me directly at

and there are many passages which may be viewed from several different perspectives.

About stuff you might not like: I recall many years ago when I loaned a challenging book about Christian economics[3] to a friend. When he returned it, I asked him what he thought. His response was, "I didn't like it. It was really good. But I didn't like it."

It is actually good for us to receive and process inputs that challenge our comfort zone. Not that we should blindly accept every wind of doctrine that blows our way. But we should examine things carefully and thoroughly so that we can let the good stuff influence us, even when (like a new pair of hiking boots) it might feel uncomfortable at first.

Jesus said that "Man does not live by bread alone, but by every word that proceeds from the mouth of God. So the message of the Kingdom is food for thought. For this reason, most sections of this book end with thought-provoking questions to help you get chewing. These questions are meant to help you start thinking about how to live in this very different sort of Kingdom in your every day life. I pray that you will find it to be a balanced and nurturing diet.

---

vandre@barbeint.no rather than criticizing me in public fora. Rather than having promoted some heresy, I have most likely simply failed to communicate my thoughts in a clear and balanced manner.

3 Sider, Ronald, *Rich Christians in an Age of Hunger*, InterVarsity Press, 1977

The Kingdom of Heaven is like...

One Sabbath morning a couple thousand years ago,[4] Jesus and his friends were on their way to the gathering in the local synagogue. Perhaps they hadn't had time to eat breakfast, because as they were walking through the grain fields some of them began to pluck and eat of the grain. It didn't take long before some self-appointed guardians of the rules began to criticize this unorthodox behavior: The Sabbath is a day of rest, and people shouldn't be doing the work of plucking grain even though they might be hungry. A conflict arose.

Once they got to the synagogue, these religious leaders brought forward a man whose hand was shriveled. They challenged Jesus as to whether or not it was OK, according to their Law, for someone to be healed on the Sabbath. Jesus took the challenge and healed the man – which, not surprisingly, raised the level of conflict. The religious leaders, in their fury over the fact that Jesus valued insignificant (in their eyes) people more than he valued their rules, went out to lay plans for putting Jesus to death. After all, according to their understanding, anyone who blatantly violated God's Law like that was subject to the wrath of God and deserved to die.

Meanwhile, Jesus left the synagogue. Crowds of people followed him and he healed all who were ill among them.

---

4   Matthew 12

The people were ecstatic, but the religious leaders were offended. So, in order to justify themselves, they accused Jesus of doing these apparently good things through the power of the evil one. After all, by their logic, the Holy One of Israel wouldn't be breaking his own rules about the Sabbath.

Jesus challenged their logic: A kingdom divided against itself is powerless. How then could the evil one be a party to delivering people from the oppression of the evil one? But their rage and offense at this uneducated and unqualified "teacher" prevented these religious leaders from understanding what Jesus was talking about. Seemingly untouched by all of the miracles which had taken place that day, they demanded that Jesus validate his authority by showing them a sign. But Jesus replied that any sign he could give would be beyond their understanding.

> *But He answered and said to them, "An evil and adulterous generation craves for a sign; and yet no sign will be given to it but the sign of Jonah the prophet; for just as Jonah was three days and three nights in the belly of the sea monster, so will the Son of Man be three days and three nights in the heart of the earth. The men of Nineveh will stand up with this generation at the judgment, and will condemn it because they repented at the preaching of Jonah; and behold, something greater than Jonah is here. The Queen of the South will rise up with this generation at the judgment and will condemn it, because she came from the ends of the earth to hear the wisdom of Solomon; and behold, something greater than Solomon is here." (Matthew 12:39-42 NASB)*

In other words, Jesus was saying that their oppressive, rules-based and judgment-based mindset blinded them from being able to comprehend what he was talking about.

At that point, Jesus began telling stories. Many of these stories (or parables) began with a phrase such as "The Kingdom of Heaven is like…" Stories of this kind are designed to illustrate something, and Jesus' parables were meant to illustrate one or more aspects of what he referred to as the Kingdom of Heaven or the Kingdom of God.

His listeners understood much more fully than we might today, just what a kingdom is. At the time, their country had been conquered and was being oppressed by a powerful foreign empire. And yet, in their own history there had been many mighty and glorious kings, so they longed to see their own kingdom re-established. Therefore, when they heard the phrase Kingdom of God, they probably assumed they had a pretty good idea what Jesus was talking about.

And yet, something didn't quite fit. The stories Jesus told were set in circumstances familiar to his listeners and often involved simple events. At the same time they were loaded with inferences and parallels that could be quite confounding, especially if one tried to hammer them into the common understanding of what a kingdom is.

When Jesus told his disciples, "the knowledge of the secrets of the Kingdom of Heaven has been given to you, but not to them,"[5] it can be seen in light of Jesus' statement to Nicodemus that "no-one can see the

---

5   Matthew 13:11

Kingdom of God unless he is born again."[6] In other words, it takes a re-born, regenerated, renewed mind under the influence and insight of the Holy Spirit to see the Kingdom of God clearly.

When Jesus told parables to the crowds, it was with a double purpose. For people who haven't experienced the transformation of mind to see with a Kingdom perspective, parables can help to prepare the soil, remove the veil and open the minds of the listeners to these hidden realities. At the same time, if a Kingdom truth is revealed plainly, then the hearer is responsible to accept or reject the word of the Lord. By alluding to these truths in parables, Jesus protected, in a sense, those whose hearts weren't yet ready for these Kingdom truths from taking on that responsibility prematurely, while at the same time planting a desire to see into the Kingdom.

And yet, for those who are able to see into the Kingdom of Heaven, the parables of Jesus give a wealth of insight into the workings of this very different sort of Kingdom. So one goal of this book is to help you get a different sort of view on some of these parables.

One of the challenges when looking closely at a parable is discerning the parts of the parable that illustrate some truth from the parts that simply provide the framework for the illustration. It can be a mistake to push the illustration too far, because the illustration is not itself the reality it illustrates, and at some point it will fail to represent the reality accurately. For example, I have many times wondered how the prodigal son's father could have failed in his fathering to the degree that his sons so misunderstood his nature, and I conclude that it

---

6 John 3:3

is at this point the illustration breaks down: The parable is not about fathering skills, but about the nature of a good father. And so, in order to make the story work in the setting at hand, this apparent inconsistency exists. I believe, however, it would be wrong to stretch the parable to the conclusion that the nature of God includes the distance and unknowableness that appear to be the starting point of that story. But more on that later.

Another issue surrounds the question of what, where and when is this Kingdom of Heaven. The word kingdom may lead some to think of a political institution. Others may tie New Testament usage of the word kingdom to the millenial kingdom mentioned in Revelation 20. Still others may think that the Kingdom of Heaven is the place they will go to after they die. In this book, I have written from the perspective that the Kingdom of Heaven is near at hand, in our midst, today; and that we who are citizens of that Kingdom are called to infuse the culture of that Kingdom into the society in which we live, here and now. More on that later, as well.

> *"Therefore everyone who hears these words of mine and puts them into practice is like a wise man who built his house on the rock. The rain came down, the streams rose, and the winds blew and beat against that house; yet it did not fall, because it had its foundation on the rock. But everyone who hears these words of mine and does not put them into practice is like a foolish man who built his house on sand. The rain came down, the streams rose, and the winds blew and beat against that house, and it fell with a great crash."* (Matthew 7:24-27)

The parables of Jesus are catalysts for shifting paradigms. If we are to really get a grip on this very different sort of Kingdom, then we will have to change the way we think. And probably more than once. If we don't, then we will end up not putting into practice the words of Jesus.

The difference between a stable and secure life and a life of fear, worry and insecurity is found in putting the message of the Kingdom into practice in your own life. In other words, you are embarking on a journey through the parables of Jesus, which ought to result in some changes in how you think, walk and live. It may, at times, seem to be uncharted territory. But it is an adventurous journey into the Kingdom of a very good King.

The King

A Place to Belong

Much of the teaching and lifestyle of Jesus can be summed up in his statement: "The Kingdom of God has come near. Repent and believe the good news!"[7] Or rather (as I might rewrite it), Jesus was saying: "I have got some really good news for you, but you need to change the way you think about God and his Kingdom or you won't be able to grasp it."

The Jewish culture into which Jesus was born viewed God as holy, unapproachable, demanding and perhaps a bit angry; none of which seemed to be very inviting or comfortable for ordinary people in their daily lives. So when Jesus proclaimed that the Kingdom of God was coming near, it might not have seemed like such good news. But then Jesus started painting a very different picture of this Kingdom's King than they had expected. It was a disruptive message, and it was challenged at nearly every turn by those in established positions of leadership.

On one such occasion, the Pharisees and scribes criticized Jesus for accepting and mingling with "sinners." When Jesus heard this, he told three stories[8] in quick succession. These stories were about a sheep which had gotten lost, a coin that was missing and a son who went away; three parables with several things in common:

---

7   Mark 1:15
8   Luke 15. Each of these three stories is covered in more detail later in the book, so I have quoted them there rather than here. You may find it helpful to stop and read through Luke 15 before going on.

- Something valuable went missing from where it belonged
- The owner's desire was to see the missing thing restored
- When restoration took place, there was great rejoicing

One thing the Pharisees failed to see was that the "tax collectors and sinners" who gathered around Jesus actually *belonged* to this Kingdom he was talking about. Perhaps these "sinners" didn't understand it consciously, but there was something about the Kingdom culture which surrounded Jesus that they found attractive and inviting. They were experiencing a touch of that place from which they had gone missing, that place where they belonged.

In English, the word *belong* has a couple of different meanings. For example, in the case of the lost sheep we could say that the sheep belongs to its owner. Or we could say that the sheep belongs in its home. Both are true, but they have substantially different implications for how the sheep would relate to being lost.[9]

A sheep may know their master primarily in terms of control. For the most part, the owner decides where they will go, how often they will get their hair cut, and when they will end up on someone's dinner table. The owner doesn't even (so it would seem) provide for their basic needs, but turns them loose to forage for their own food. With such a perspective, belonging might feel constraining while getting lost may seem like getting free.

---
9 In order to illustrate a point here, it may be that I am giving sheep more credit for logical and emotional thinking than they actually deserve.

If, however, the sheep relates to its master as a caregiver, one who creates a sense of belonging where there is safety and rest, then being lost is not a good thing at all. A sheep in a pen might view the fence as a boundary holding them in or a line of defense holding chaos and danger out; primarily depending on their understanding of their master.

In these stories of something that was missing from where it belonged, the owner (who represents God the Father) was passionate about restoration. This was not due to the owner's need for control, but is rather a result of how highly he values that which was lost. The owner's heart longs to bring about the best for that which has gone missing. The nature of Father God is to see things restored to where they belong, so that they come into the place of rest for which they were created, and so that joy may be released.

> *For God so loved the world that he gave his one and only son, ... For God did not send his Son into the world to condemn the world, but to save the world through him. (John 3:16a, 17)*

In the first two stories, there was something missing from its owner. However, in the third (and most detailed) of these stories, a son was restored to his father. Restoration between children and fathers is a core longing of the Father who so loves the world. Father God has been longing and working to see his children restored ever since they went missing in the Garden of Eden. This is clear in the final words of the Old Testament:

> *Remember the law of Moses My servant, even the statutes and ordinances which I commanded him*

> *in Horeb for all Israel. Behold, I am going to send you Elijah the prophet before the coming of the great and terrible day of the Lord. And he will restore the hearts of the fathers to their children, and the hearts of the children to their fathers, lest I come and smite the land with a curse. (Malachi 4:4-6 NASB)*

Some 400 years later, the angel Gabriel appeared to a priest named Zacharias to tell him about the son that he would soon father:

> *And he will turn back many of the sons of Israel to the Lord their God. And it is he who will go as a forerunner before Him in the spirit and power of Elijah, to turn the hearts of the fathers back to the children, and the disobedient to the attitude of the righteous, so as to make ready a people prepared for the Lord. (Luke 1:16-17 NASB)*

Jewish culture during these 400 years had focused on the first part of Malachi's admonition. Not only did they remember the Law, but they expanded upon it and refined it so as to regulate everything and leave nothing to chance. The result, about three times as many rules as Moses had originally received in Horeb, led them to think that they could serve the Lord without approaching or knowing him.

I rather doubt that this focus on mechanically following the rules is what God meant by remembering the Law. Both Malachi's prophecy and Gabriel's message touch on a deeper issue: restoring the father-child relationship. Could it rather be that God, through Malachi, is saying something like, "Remember all those commands that made you think you could serve me from a distance?

That's not what I am looking for. No, I want to relate to you like a father again, and I want to restore you to your position as my child."

Rules and commandments bring a curse, for "cursed is he who does not confirm the words of this law by doing them."[10] And clearly the desire of the Lord, as spoken through Malachi, is to avoid the curse; and this is done through the restoration of father-child relationships – especially the relationship between God the Father and his missing children.

Remember that Jesus told these three stories in response to the accusation that he was hanging out with sinners and *accepting* them. Jesus makes it clear that he accepts sinners because they are missing from where they belong: safe at home with their Father. A central point in each of these stories is that the Father is passionate about recovering what belongs to him and restoring it to its original glory. This is redemption[11] – purchasing back what is rightfully his but has fallen into the hands of an adversary.

This becomes especially clear when the prodigal son starts to recite his rehearsed speech about no longer being worthy to be called a son. His father cuts him off abruptly. The father doesn't want to hear such lies proclaimed. Instead he orders that the son be wrapped in visible symbols of sonship as quickly as possible. There is no mistaking the father's perspective of who his son is and where he belongs.

---

10 Deuteronomy 27:26 NASB
11 See Colossians 1:13-14, 1:19-22, 2:13-14; Ephesians 1:7-8a, Romans 3:24

There is no indication of anger and no threat of punishment in any of these stories. Of course, it doesn't make much sense to punish a coin for getting lost, and it may be foolish to be angry with the sheep. But in the case of the son there was good reason (in human terms) to be angry with the son who went away and to punish him. But that didn't happen.

Jesus' point here is unmistakable: His Father is not angry with sinners. Rather, he is actively working to bring them to that place of restoration. God, in his holiness, is not allergic to sin. His Kingdom draws near so that his lost children will catch the fragrance and move into his embrace of redemption.

Look again

Let's stop and dwell on this a bit. If you don't get a clear view of who the King is and what is central to his nature, then you will misunderstand the workings of his Kingdom. The King is God. The King is a Good Father. It may just be that you need to change the way you think about this King *a whole lot*. But don't worry, this is good news.

So what are we looking at?

- You *belong* in the Kingdom. In fact, you have *always* belonged. You were created as a child of the Kingdom. It is your home and your destiny.

- You are *welcome* in the Kingdom. In fact, you are wanted there. There is nothing you have done or can do that will make you more (or less) welcome.

- The King is passionate about seeing restored to you and in you *everything* that does not yet measure up to the fullness of what he created you to be. He gave his Son to accomplish this purpose.
- The King is not angry with you. He is not disappointed with you. He is not ashamed of you. He is not going to punish you.

What does that mean in practice?

Not long ago, I was a bit careless while bicycling home from work. The wheel of my bicycle fell into a streetcar track. The bicycle stopped in its tracks (as it were), but I didn't. The result: a badly broken ankle, surgery, and weeks on crutches.

It would be natural to wonder why that happened. And our perspective of the nature of the King and what he is like will shape how we might answer that question. But if our view of the King is distorted then the conclusions we draw can be misleading or even quite damaging to our ability to see his Kingdom clearly.

Let's look at some examples:
- **Sovereign**: God Almighty is omnipotent and omniscient. But if we believe that his sovereignty is his dominant attribute, then we will view an accident of this type as part of his perfect will. That would lead us to think he *caused* the accident in order to accomplish some greater good, such as to get me to change the tempo in my life (which I have, and which has been good for me). The logical conclusion of this perspective is that I have no inherent value, other than to be a pawn which the master can use and manipulate as he desires

in order to accomplish his inscrutable plans or whims. But that perspective is a terrible misrepresentation of the nature of the King who loved the world so much that he gave *his own* Son.

- **Judge**: The Holy One of Israel is often seen as a judge. But if his holiness is his dominant attribute, then his Law and his commandments can easily become the framework for what happens to us. After all, you reap what you sow. This would lead us to think that God allowed the accident to take place in order to punish me for riding too fast or for crossing the tracks in the wrong place or for some other sin or wrong theology. Or maybe I was punished as a sign to my community or nation for some evil that has become widespread in society. This is also a distortion of the nature of the King. Jesus told these three parables about belonging, directly in response to the idea that sinners deserve punishment rather than acceptance.

- **Entitlement**: Viewing God as sovereign and a judge could also lead us to react with a spirit of entitlement. Entitlement is the feeling that the world owes me something because of who I am or what I have done. It would lead us to think something like, "God, why did you do this to me?" This is especially likely if we feel as though God owes us something for all of our service to him. This spirit builds on several lies about the nature of God: that he caused the accident, that he doesn't care about me, that he doesn't like me, that I'm not valuable, and more. It leads to bitterness, which is cancer of the soul.

- **Distant**: God in Heaven can seem very far away. We might think that our sins keep him from drawing near. Or we might think he has more important things to do than to be concerned with the details of our lives. After all, he has given us a book of principles to learn and to follow. And then, until that time he calls you or me home, we're on our own to get through the battles of this life. We might view the accident as an attack of the enemy. But God will cause it all to work out in the end, so we just need to hold out until then. This picture of the King is also a misrepresentation. His passion for restoration and his joyous celebration when restoration breaks forth speak against this distortion.

- **Father**: God is love. And as John wrote, perfect love casts out all fear, for fear has to do with punishment. Viewing the King as a loving Father means that we see him welcoming us into safety and acceptance. This perspective doesn't answer the question of *why* the accident took place. But that question becomes irrelevant in the adventure of where we go hand in hand together with the King from this time forward.

How we view the King will have a huge bearing on what we are able to see in the Kingdom. Nobody has a clearer understanding of the nature of God than Jesus, who constantly referred to God as Father. Any other starting point is a distortion.

Will not the Judge of all the Earth do right?[12]

For many of us, perhaps our biggest struggle stems from the misconception that God is first and foremost the Judge. We might have gotten this idea from the way we first heard the gospel – that we are sinners and the penalty for sin is death, but fortunately Jesus paid the penalty for us, thereby appeasing God the Judge. Although all of the facts in such a presentation of the gospel are technically true, the resulting picture which portrays God as Judge is a distortion.

There are two facets of this distortion which cloud our vision: First, although God does pass judgment, our vision is distorted if we see judgment as the dominant attribute of his nature; and second, we may well have an incorrect understanding of what it means for God to judge.

Perhaps no person has had a greater revelation of the nature of God than the apostle John. And he wrote that God is love. Now, John did not write that God is Judge or that God is righteous, or that God is holy – even though it is clear that John believed all of these things to be true about God. Rather, the revelation that John shared with us is that God *is love*, and that all of his attributes spring out of his loving nature.

And then John wrote:

> *There is no fear in love. But perfect love drives out fear, because fear has to do with punishment. The one who fears is not made perfect in love. (1 John 4:18)*

---

12   Genesis 18:25

This verse speaks directly to how we should understand God as Judge. If God is love, then his judgment will not produce fear and it is not about punishment.[13]

Now, you might react to that last statement. But take another look. Either John didn't know what he was writing about, or we need to change the way we think. Consider this: In what ways is Jesus different from God the Father? I would say none.[14] And if we are likely to think of Jesus as friend, why then would we think differently of God?

When we think of a judge, we probably think of a judge in a courtroom passing sentence over convicted wrongdoers. And then we transpose that image onto God. But John's claim that God is love shatters such an image. On the other hand, we could view a judge as the person who hands out awards in a contest.[15] This kind of a judge does not generate fear or distribute punishment.

God's judgment of the Earth is a good thing.[16] The judgment seat of Christ is for us to receive the reward which is our due.[17]

Party time

Or suppose a woman has ten silver coins and loses one. Doesn't she light a lamp, sweep the house and search carefully until she finds it? And when she

---

13　There *is* a punishment for sin, but that debt has been completely paid by the death of Jesus on the Cross. We will come back to that in a later chapter.
14　See Hebrews 1:3 and John 14:9
15　See 2 Timothy 4:8
16　For example, see Psalm 82:8, 96:13 and 98:9.
17　See 1 Corinthians 3:11-15 and 2 Corinthians 5:10.

> *finds it, she calls her friends and neighbors together and says, "Rejoice with me; I have found my lost coin." In the same way, I tell you, there is rejoicing in the presence of the angels of God over one sinner who repents. (Luke 15:8-10)*

Each of the three parables in Luke 15 ends with a party. Each time a missing item is restored to where it belongs, a party breaks out. In the Kingdom of God, restoration is not something that takes place grudgingly. Rather, the true nature of the King is shown by his unrestrained celebration of each child that finds their way back to where they belong.

The gospels tell us that Jesus frequently attended dinner parties and feasts. In fact, his detractors ridiculed Jesus as being a glutton and drunkard. And yet, Jesus said that he only did what he saw his Father doing; and the writer to the Hebrews said that Jesus was the exact representation of the nature of God.

Therefore, it is reasonable to conclude that the Father is constantly looking for opportunities to celebrate and rejoice. In fact, it was the joy set before him[18] that carried Jesus through his death on the Cross, which opened the way for our restoration to where we belong as children of our Father the King.

This is perhaps the heart of repentance. We may often think that repentance means to stop sinning and instead do righteous works. But that is a very narrow definition. To repent means to turn around, to look at things from a different perspective, to change the way you think.

---

18 See Hebrews 12:2

When Jesus came saying, "repent and believe in the gospel," he was saying that the widespread understanding of God as a stodgy old judge looking for an opportunity to condemn you for breaking a rule was a total misrepresentation. Instead, he painted a picture of a Father longing to welcome his children home in an atmosphere of celebration.

Food for thought

Try to visualize Father God celebrating you. What does that look like to you? Does it make you feel uncomfortable? If so, why? What is Jesus saying in these parables to reassure you that you belong in that place of celebration?

Does it feel more "right" to you to view God as a judge than as a father? Does it feel comfortable? Does God look different to you than Jesus does?

How do you react to the idea that God is not angry with you? Does such a claim lead you to respond with anger or indignation? Does it frighten you? Or does it make you feel welcome home? Why?

The Prodigal Son's Father

The parable of the prodigal son has always been a favorite of mine. Especially after Keith Green's *Prodigal Son Suite* was released in the early 1980's, I have at times been overwhelmed by the demonstration of unconditional love and acceptance shown by the father when he first sees his son returning home.

The story is actually quite simple: a son rejects his home and family, squanders his inheritance, and after learning some hard lessons decides to return home. Although he considers himself to be invaluable and unforgivable, his father surprises him with acceptance and value.

Amazing! Too good to be true. And totally unfair.

As we shall see, this simple story of a father's love, acceptance and forgiveness contains a wealth of insight into the nature of God our King as a Good Father. But first, let's look at the story as it was recorded by Luke.

> *There was a man who had two sons. The younger one said to his father, "Father, give me my share of the estate." So he divided his property between them.*
>
> *Not long after that, the younger son got together all he had, set off for a distant country and there squandered his wealth in wild living. After he had spent everything, there was a severe famine in that whole country, and he began to be in need. So he went and hired himself out to a citizen of that country, who sent him to his fields to feed pigs. He*

longed to fill his stomach with the pods that the pigs were eating, but no one gave him anything.

When he came to his senses, he said, "How many of my father's hired servants have food to spare, and here I am starving to death! I will set out and go back to my father and say to him: Father, I have sinned against Heaven and against you. I am no longer worthy to be called your son; make me like one of your hired servants." So he got up and went to his father.

But while he was still a long way off, his father saw him and was filled with compassion for him; he ran to his son, threw his arms around him and kissed him.

The son said to him, "Father, I have sinned against Heaven and against you. I am no longer worthy to be called your son."

But the father said to his servants, "Quick! Bring the best robe and put it on him. Put a ring on his finger and sandals on his feet. Bring the fattened calf and kill it. Let's have a feast and celebrate. For this son of mine was dead and is alive again; he was lost and is found." So they began to celebrate.

Meanwhile, the older son was in the field. When he came near the house, he heard music and dancing. So he called one of the servants and asked him what was going on. "Your brother has come," he replied, "and your father has killed the fattened calf because he has him back safe and sound."

The older brother became angry and refused to go in. So his father went out and pleaded with him.

But he answered his father, "Look! All these years I've been slaving for you and never disobeyed your orders. Yet you never gave me even a young goat so I could celebrate with my friends. But when this son of yours who has squandered your property with prostitutes comes home, you kill the fattened calf for him!"

"My son," the father said, "you are always with me, and everything I have is yours. But we had to celebrate and be glad, because this brother of yours was dead and is alive again; he was lost and is found." (Luke 15:11-32)

Grace

This story starts out with a simple request: the younger son asks his father for his share of the inheritance. At first glance, that may not seem any worse than a bit of youthful foolishness. But it was, in that culture, a mortal sin.

One of the ten commandments, the first commandment with a promise,[19] is to honor your father and your mother. The promise tied to the commandment, to live long and well in the land, demonstrates that there is a cause and effect relationship between the degree to which we honor the generation(s) that preceded us, and the degree of blessing that we will experience in our time and in our own lives. Perhaps this is because dishonoring our parents is also dishonoring Father God, the source of all blessing.

---

19 Ephesians 6:1-3, Deuteronomy 5:16

I grew up in a time of social upheaval. The values of my parents' generation, as evidenced in racial discrimination, rampant materialism and the war in Vietnam, were rejected by my generation. We thought that by rejecting the evils of the establishment we were building a future of peace, love and freedom. But the fruit of that rejection turned out to be the widespread adoption of values such as rebellion, arrogance and immorality.

In American culture (and I suspect also in many other western cultures) we lost respect for authority. In my childhood there was a general sense of respect for positions of authority, even though the person holding the office may not have deserved that respect. But as I grew up, that respect waned. Today, we see a multitude of examples in the media where people in public positions are treated disrespectfully, even though their actions are honorable. And with that cultural shift, we have pretty much lost the ability to honor our parents' generation.

I doubt that, as a culture, we truly understand how great a price we have paid. Among other things, that price included the loss of a cultural understanding of honor. Neither do we value honoring age or wisdom, nor do we realize how much potential blessing we have wasted as a result of having abandoned that value.

Honor was a big deal in the culture of Jesus' day. At times, defending or restoring honor could be considered more important than the lives of people. In fact, the Law of Moses required that a rebellious son be stoned to death by the men of the community. So, dishonoring a parent was no inconsequential matter.

> *If someone has a stubborn and rebellious son who does not obey his father and mother and will not listen to them when they discipline him, his father and mother shall take hold of him and bring him to the elders at the gate of his town. They shall say to the elders, "This son of ours is stubborn and rebellious. He will not obey us. He is a glutton and a drunkard." Then all the men of his town are to stone him to death. You must purge the evil from among you. All Israel will hear of it and be afraid.*
> *(Deuteronomy 21:18-21)*

Such is the younger son's starting point in this story. Not only did he treat his father disrespectfully, but by demanding his share of the inheritance he was in essence saying that he considered his father as good as dead.

And then this son squandered his inheritance in wild living. In other words, he played the glutton and drunkard. Clearly, the younger son's behavior was unforgivable. According to the Law of the day, he deserved the death penalty.[20]

And for just that reason, the behavior of his father is worth our close examination. First of all, the father broke the rules by not bringing his son before the elders at the gate. Despite his son's shameful behavior, the father's love for his son led him to protect his son from the penalty that was his due.

---

20 It could possibly be argued that the younger son did not actually rebel against his father, but only sought his independence. In my opinion, that is likely not the case here. His having squandered the inheritance in wild living fits with the description of rebellion from Deuteronomy 21. And, a unilateral declaration of independence is, in essence, a statement of rebellion.

And when the father saw his son returning, he ran to meet him. No doubt, one reason that he ran was to embrace the son that he so loved and missed. But another reason was that if he wasn't the first person to receive his son, some man of the town might see him and initiate the penalty of death by stoning which the Law required.

When Jesus told this story, it was in response to an accusation made by the religious leaders of the day, who considered themselves guardians of the Law. They complained about the fact that Jesus was accepting and having fellowship with sinners, rather than treating them with the attitude of contempt and condemnation that, according to the religious system, was their due for being rule-breakers.

Jesus told this story to illustrate to these religious leaders that their understanding of God was quite wrong. The father in this story illustrates important facets of the nature of our Heavenly Father, especially that the heart of God is for grace and forgiveness, even to the extent of violating his own Law.

The Mosaic Law is an incomplete and imperfect picture of the heart of God. The Law illuminates the holiness of God and the fallen state of mankind. It encompasses the glory and power of the Almighty God, but you have to dig pretty deep to see his Father heart or his nature of love and grace. The prodigal son's father brings balance to the equation by preferring to walk in grace while judgment in accordance with righteousness would have been the more politically correct option.

The younger son understood righteousness. He knew that his life was forfeit. And in his desperation (no self-respecting Jewish man would consider sharing the food of an unclean animal such as a pig!) he decided to apply for some measure of mercy from his father. He knew that he could not expect to be received, he was well aware of the rules which he had violated. He had probably been kicking himself in the rear for months, telling himself what a terrible person he was and how he deserved to be treated as the scum of the Earth.

And the older son understood righteousness. He knew that he was a faithful and obedient member of the family. And therefore, he considered himself better than his brother. We can imagine that he was perhaps a bit smug, and maybe even rejoiced a bit over the just desserts that had become his brother's lot in life. He might even have considered his brother accursed.

But neither of these young men understood their father. The Father has no pleasure in the death of the wicked[21] but rather his delight is to show mercy.[22] When he saw his younger son from afar, clothed in rags and smelling like a pig, he responded in accord with the core of his being. He forgot the transgressions and poured out grace.

First, he ran to embrace his son. This is particularly significant. Often, when we think about God the Father, we are struck by his awesome holiness, and rightly so. We may think that this Holy God cannot tolerate the presence of sin, as if holiness were a fragile thing. But in this illustration of his Father, Jesus presents us with a different view: The overwhelming love of the father for his son leads him to wrap his arms around this filthy, rag-covered, swine-smelling wreck of a young man, and

---

21 Ezekiel 18:23, 18:32, 33:11
22 Micah 7:18

pour love into him. However much the Father may hate sin, it is not evident in how he demonstrates his love for his son. No amount of human sinfulness can quench the love of the Father.

And then, as quickly as possible, he clothed his son in a robe (symbolizing righteousness), a ring (royalty) and sandals (riches). Not only did he say that his son who had been dead was now alive again. But he also demonstrated through these concrete acts that this young man was accepted as his son. He wasn't going to let this son, or anyone else for that matter, exercise judgment or punishment where he had chosen grace.

It must have grieved the heart of the father greatly when the older brother reacted the way he did. How was it that this older brother, who had been a faithful son and who had watched his younger brother bring pain and grief to his father, still failed to understand his father's love? The father undoubtedly wanted to share with his faithful son the overwhelming joy of the younger brother's "resurrection," but the older brother appears to have favored condemnation.

Think of the missed opportunity that lay available to the older brother. He and his father could have stood together as the hosts of a great celebration. He could have stood in a position of honor and begun to walk in the destiny for which his father was preparing him: being a man of grace rather than servant of the rules. But despite so many years in the presence of the father, he had failed to understand his father's heart.

Speaking with grace

In our own time, a lot of biblical rules are being broken as behaviors that were once considered to be morally unthinkable are instead becoming socially acceptable. For example, in previous generations the church has looked upon things such as divorce, sexual freedom, abortion, homosexual marriage, and euthanasia[23] as immoral; and yet in our generation they are becoming common and acceptable. These things have not become "normal" overnight. Rather they are changes that come about as Western society moves away from it's Christian heritage – a process that includes cultural manipulation and political battle.

As part of this political battle, voices will arise to condemn the change that leads to the social acceptance of yet another broken rule. Our call as Christians to be salt and light in our community makes it important for us to clearly speak for what is true and right and pure. We must not resign ourselves to accepting the spread of unrighteousness.

However, if our zeal for righteousness leads us to behave like the older brother, then we have failed to understand our Father's love. The Father would much rather see us stand together with him in celebration of the restoration and homecoming of a beloved child, than be forced to leave the party because of our angry insistence on condemnation.

One of the images etched into my memory is of a group of people protesting homosexual marriage with banners

---

23 It is not my intent to condemn anyone who is divorced or has had an abortion or whatever. I bring these issues up primarily as examples of societal change.

carrying slogans like "God hates fags." It is inevitably these kinds of images that make the news and influence popular understanding of what the Kingdom of God looks like.

Can you imagine what great sorrow the Father experiences when we so misrepresent his nature of love and grace in our attempts to defend his standard of righteousness? And it is perhaps even more disappointing to him when his children fail to understand his nature and thereby fail to grow in his likeness and walk into the destiny for which he has called us. I suspect that this disappointment[24] is a far greater sorrow to the Lord than the fact that "prodigal children," who are not (yet) called by his name, are breaking his rules.

> *Let your speech always be with grace, seasoned, as it were, with salt, so that you may know how you should respond to each person. (Colossians 4:6 NASB)*

Jonah

The prodigal son story ends with a conversation that reminds me of the story of Jonah. Jonah was a prophet whom God asked to go to a foreign city and proclaim a message of impending doom.

Jonah saw two problems with this assignment:

---

[24] This is not to imply that the Father is disappointed to have us as his children, but rather that there is sorrow over the grace and redemption which could have been demonstrated to a lost world, but isn't.

- The people of Nineveh were foreigners and enemies, so he didn't see any real value in their salvation. They were, in his view, accursed enemies of the people of God.
- Jonah knew God to be a gracious and compassionate God, slow to anger and abounding in love, a God who relents from sending calamity.[25]

Therefore, since Jonah feared that the people in Nineveh would receive his message and change their ways, he tried to run away. His preference was for this heathen people to get the judgment they deserved for their ungodly ways. That way they would no longer be able to bring shame or sorrow upon his own people.

But God was true to his nature. He wanted the Ninevites to hear the message and he wanted to demonstrate his grace and compassion. The interesting part of Jonah's story is how far God went in order to make Jonah a part of the process.

When Jonah ran off, God could have easily enough looked for another prophet to carry the message. But like a father intent on transmitting his core values to his son, God put Jonah through the bowels of the fish, as it were, to clearly demonstrate to Jonah the importance of grace and love in the heart of God.

The Jonah story and the conversation between the prodigal son's father and his older son touch on the same message. In essence, Father is saying: "Don't you get it? I am all about love. There is nothing that brings me more delight than when a person whom I love turns to me. This is my nature. And I so desire for it to be your

---

25 Jonah 4:2

destiny. Won't you abandon your hardness and learn of me?"

Food for thought

To what extent do you understand the grace that has been given to you? Is it your heart that evildoers will experience undeserved grace? Do your words carry a fragrance of grace? Are you growing into your calling as an image of your gracious Father?

What is the difference between grace as something you receive and grace as the core of God's nature?

Inheritance

I once knew a man. In his youth he married a single mother and adopted her son. But, after some years, that marriage ended in divorce. Although he tried to maintain a relationship with his adopted son, that boy's ties were understandably closer to his mother. Later this man had a relationship to another single mother and, although they never formalized the relationship with marriage, he played very much the role of father to her children. Eventually, his health faltered and he passed away, leaving a real but informal family in addition to his one legal heir. Unfortunately, some difficulties arose at the time of his funeral, as the adopted son contested the relationship of the informal family. It seemed as though the son was more concerned about securing the inheritance for himself, than about the loss experienced by those who were close to his adopted father. In the midst of the grief and pain that this situation bore, it became clear to me how tragic it is when a son has a closer relationship to the inheritance than he has to his father.

And yet, that appears to be very much the case in the story of the prodigal son. In fact, it looks like both sons were more able to relate to the inheritance than they were to their father; but they related to it in different ways.

The younger son's demand to receive his share of the inheritance while his father yet lived expresses how little value he had for the life of his father. As previously mentioned, he was saying something like, "Give me what I've got coming, because you might as well be dead, as far as I am concerned." It was a disgraceful act that, according to the norms of the day, was unforgivable.

But the older brother, though afraid to break so many of society's rules and expectations, does not appear to have been so different. His complaint to his father is quite revealing:

> *Look! All these years I've been slaving for you and never disobeyed your orders. Yet you never gave me even a young goat so I could celebrate with my friends. (Luke 15:29)*

Here, he refers to his relationship to his father as one of slavery. He clearly neither understood his father's nature nor his own position as an heir. He saw only the work to be done in order to some day claim the inheritance without the disgrace that his younger brother had brought down on himself.

Sadly, this same tragedy is widespread in the church today, influencing our preaching, evangelism, prayer and even our worship.

The preaching of the early church was focused on the crucifixion of Jesus.[26] His perfect offering that fulfilled all of the requirements of the Law and tore open the veil that had separated people from the Father's love were fundamental elements of the gospel that Peter and Paul preached.

That is a far cry from the simple message of salvation that we often hear from evangelists today: that, if only one asks Jesus into their heart, they will get to go to Heaven. Yes, there is a truth here, but the focus is all wrong. It puts the focus on the inheritance rather than on relationship to the Father.

Think about it. If my primary motivation for following Christ is getting to Heaven (or avoiding the wrath of hell), how will that affect my relationship to God? How will it influence my understanding of what is dear to His heart? Will I even be able to relate to him as Father?

Often, we hear the gospel presented mainly in judicial terms. All have sinned; the wages of sin are death; Jesus paid the price; you need to get your case in order with God. This approach to the gospel portrays God as Judge (which is true, but only one facet of the truth) and puts us in a fearful position in relationship to the Judge. When this Judge meets us with grace, cleansing us from all sin, it is a truly wonderful salvation! But what is the fruit of a salvation that fails to develop a relationship to the Father? I think it is evident in the largely unchanged lives of believers who have received grace upon grace without having grown to maturity in a family likeness to their Father.

---

26 For example, see 1 Corinthians 1:23, 1 Corinthians 11:26, Galatians 3:2

The preaching of Peter stands in contrast:

> *Repent, then, and turn to God, so that your sins may be wiped out, that times of refreshing may come from the Lord, and that he may send the Christ, who has been appointed for you – even Jesus. (Acts 3:19-20)*

First of all, he says: "Repent." In the previous verses, Peter pointed out that his listeners had been complicit in the crucifixion of Jesus. Their complicity had come to pass as a crowd had been stirred up to demand punishment for apparently breaking the rules of an angry and demanding God. When Peter said, "Repent," he was in essence saying "Change the way you think." It was not so much "Repent and stop sinning," as it was "You need to change the way you think about God: He is not an angry Judge but a loving Father."

The remainder of verses 19-20 are primarily relational: turn to God, times of refreshing from the Lord, the Christ appointed for you. Peter makes it clear that this new life[27] is all about having a relationship to Father God. The great revelation here is that God is neither angry nor demanding, because the requirements of the Law have been fulfilled by the crucifixion of the Christ.

The first century believers faced skepticism and persecution, and yet the believers of that time had counted the cost and found that following Jesus was worth it. This wasn't just because they were holding out until they could get to Heaven. No, this life as a child of the Father and a brother or sister of the Son and a container for the Holy Spirit was really, really good. In fact, it was so good that there were even some who

---

27   Acts 5:20

believed and followed even though they doubted that there would be any resurrection of the dead.[28] Although Paul needed to correct their misunderstanding about the inheritance, it still points to something very healthy in that their focus was on their present relationship to the triune God.

Worship

> *Yet a time is coming and has now come when the true worshipers will worship the Father in the Spirit and in truth, for they are the kind of worshipers the Father seeks. (John 4:23)*

In my own experience, one of the most fruitful ways to further develop my relationship with the Father is through worship. Worship is much more than singing songs or carrying out the elements of a worship service. Still, for many of us, singing songs of worship and praise is a substantial part of the practice of worshiping.

So what picture gets painted if the content of our songs is primarily focused on what Jesus has done for us? Don't misunderstand me here. There is nothing wrong with a song of joy and thanksgiving for the overwhelming salvation that is ours, or for its many benefits. But it is the Father who seeks worshipers, so a significant part of true worship is expressions to our Father of how great and magnificent he *is* and how much we love and appreciate *Him*. If the bulk of our communication to him through worship is mostly about the inheritance (what he gives us or will give us), then we are in danger of failing to develop a healthy relationship with the Father.

---

28   1 Corinthians 15:12-19

When Moses, in his meeting with God at the burning bush, asked what name he should use to identify the God of their fathers, the name was *I Am*. In Hebrew culture, a name was not just a label but an expression of identity. By calling himself *I Am*, God was saying that his identity is not based in what he does, has done or will do but in who he is here and now. It is a tragic misrepresentation of his nature to understand, value or relate to him primarily through his actions.

There is, as far as I know, only one thing that the almighty, all-encompassing, creator God cannot gain for himself through his own efforts: people who choose to love him of their own free will. It stands to reason that such expressions of love are highly valued by the Father. True worshipers will express this kind of love and intimacy through their songs, words and actions. A style of worship that expresses our love of Father God, that praises his character and exalts him is, I believe, far more pleasing to him than one that focuses mostly on what we receive from him.

Ownership

While we are on the subject of inheritance, it is also worth looking at how the father and his sons understood ownership.

Both of the sons, each in his own way, understood ownership in a very different manner from their father. The younger son said, "give me my share" and the older son said "you never gave me even a young goat." These statements indicate that the sons understood ownership in terms of control. They wanted things in order to use them as they wished. Although the older son didn't demand his inheritance ahead of time, he looked forward to the day when he would be in control of the family assets.

It is the owner who decides what will be done with the things they own. In the eyes of these two young men (and perhaps most of us), the inheritance is a bunch of resources to be used. Once they gain ownership and are free to use it as they like, the inheritance will likely be spent on their comfort and desires.

Their father, however, sees things in a broader perspective. You get a hint of this when the father goes ahead and divides the estate even though he probably knew all too well that his younger son lacked the maturity to manage his resources well. For the father, creating opportunities to grow in maturity (despite the risk of failure) was more highly valued than making sure his sons made the right choices.

The revealing statement comes in the father's conversation with his older son: "you are always with me, and everything I have is yours; but we had to celebrate." Part of what I see the father saying here is that his view of ownership was not so much about controlling how his estate would be run, as it was about making resources available to his sons so that they would have the opportunity to grow into their destiny – even though they may choose to waste that opportunity. In other words, the father's focus as owner was freedom and blessing rather than control.

Food for thought

What is your inheritance as a child of the King? How do you relate to the inheritance? What specific things can you start doing to grow more into the likeness of Father God? What motivates your communication with the Father, and how do you express it?

Do you see God as controlling or empowering? What does it mean to say that he values free will?

Servanthood

The older brother seems to have surmised that the road to his father's heart was through service. He was a faithful son, but his reaction to his younger brother's return shows that the basis for his faithfulness was something less than an alignment to the heart of his father.

Though he was a son, the older brother viewed his own life as that of a servant. Service is a very different thing from sonship, even though they may look quite similar at the outset.[29]

A servant is called to obedience to the master. His obedience is regulated primarily through a system of reward or punishment. If the servant carries out his duties in a noteworthy manner then he may receive some reward. If he fails to obey then he will be punished. Usually, the fear of punishment becomes the driving motivator for the servant. If the rewards are few then he learns, above all else, how to avoid pain. The result will be performance just good enough to avoid the pain, but little more.

---

29 Galatians 4:1

And when the threat of pain is removed there is no longer any motivator to perform well, which often results in unwise choices. In fact, this may be just what happened with the younger brother. He cut himself off from an environment of discipline, without having developed in himself the maturity to make wise choices. With his pockets full of money, it was easy to let pain-avoidance govern his actions. But his wealth was gone long before he had gained the maturity to let his life be guided by something more than the avoidance of pain.

Sonship, however, is another matter. Growing in sonship begins with a form of training where reward and punishment are a part of the picture. But, unlike the servant who only hears the instructions of his master, a son has access to the father and learns mostly by imitating his father. The goal of sonship is not so much to accomplish tasks as it is to transmit values and foster maturity. In a healthy father-son relationship, the son will not only learn to avoid punishment, but he will also learn to understand and follow his father's heart. Sonship then becomes a matter of seeing and carrying forward a vision toward a destiny; ideally one that will again be passed on to the next generation.[30]

In other words, a servant knows what he is supposed to do and may know what the master wants done. But a son knows his father's heart[31] and he walks with a view to the future.

---

30 This topic of sonship is much larger than scope of this book. I pray that you will wish to pursue it further. I recommend checking out the schools and resources of Fatherheart Ministries (www.fatherheart.net). I also recommend the book "No Longer Orphans: Journey into the Father's Heart" by James Macchi.
31 John 15:15

> *Jesus, knowing that the Father had given all things into His hands, and that He had come forth from God and was going back to God, got up from supper, and laid aside His garments; and taking a towel, He girded Himself. Then He poured water into the basin, and began to wash the disciples' feet and to wipe them with the towel with which He was girded. (John 13:3-5 NASB)*

A son is not a servant. But a son will often choose to serve. However, a son who serves with a servant identity is not walking in sonship. Jesus frequently acted as a servant of God and a servant to people. But he didn't serve because he was a servant; he served with a clear understanding of his identity as a son. Likewise, Paul also referred to himself at times as the slave of Christ. But Paul's understanding of his servant role had its roots in his identity as a child of God his Father.

When God the Father sent God the Son to walk among us as a man, it was with a purpose. Or as Jesus said, he came not to do his own will but to do the will of his Father. That purpose was *not* that Jesus would gather some more servants into the Kingdom of Heaven. The King already has plenty of servants. Rather, Jesus' goal was to bring many sons and daughters to glory.[32] Just as the prodigal son's father was longing for the return of his son, Father God longs for his sons and daughters to return to him.

Good versus best

The words of the younger son reveal an interesting insight: 'How many of my father's hired servants have food to spare ... Father, ... make me like one of your hired

---
32 Hebrews 2:10

servants.' Obviously, servanthood in his father's house was better than his current situation. But it is also clear that his father's servants were pretty well off. In other words, life was pretty good being a servant of this man.

And therein lies a huge challenge. Very likely, the older son was pretty happy being a servant in the house of his father. His needs were met and there was plenty in the estate. His father was good to his servants, so punishments may well have been few and far between. Why rock the boat?

In fact, it is easier to be a servant. All a servant needs to do to be acceptable is to follow instructions. No burden of responsibilities, no weight of decisions to make, just do as you're told and everything works out fine.

One principle I learned in my youth is that it is the good things in life that keep us from the things that are best for us. Or as Oswald Chambers put it: "The greatest enemy of the life with God is not sin, but the good that is not good enough."[33]

Because relating to his father as a servant was a pretty good life, the older son never actually took the steps to move from a relationship of service to the fullness of sonship that was available to him.

Likewise, I suspect that there are many in the church today who have discovered that it is good to be a servant of our God. And yet perhaps they find that servant role to be sufficiently comfortable, so that they don't move through it into sonship. This is most certainly a source of

---

33 Chambers, Oswald, *Knowing Not Wither*. ©1934, Oswald Chambers Publications Association, Chapter 5, Section 2.

sorrow to the Father. We were not created only to serve him, but primarily created for fellowship with him.

Servanthood versus sonship

In order to gain a clear perspective of the nature of the King, we need to be looking from the right position. Looking from a position of servanthood distorts our view of the King. Looking from a perspective of sonship brings his nature into focus.

Sonship differs from service in a number of ways:

Acceptance
- A servant works to gain acceptance by his performance. His value is dependent on how well he meets expectations. He may end up constantly striving to be good enough and he may live under the fear of being found wanting.

  There are many believers who struggle with acceptance. They may profess a salvation by grace, but in practice they still tend to measure their own value by their ability to walk in holiness. They may think of themselves as sinners and weigh themselves down with self-condemnation. Deep down they may live in fear that they will not manage to stay clean enough to pass the judgment seat of Christ.

- A son's value is inherent in his position as a son. He *is* accepted. There is nothing he can do to be loved by the Father more, or less, than he is already greatly loved.

A son is not a sinner. He was a sinner, but the old man was put to death in the waters of baptism.[34] A son is a son from birth. That position is not dependent on anything we do or fail to do. Our acceptance rests completely on what Jesus did on the Cross.

Guidance

- A servant follows the rules. A servant has no vested interest in the matters of his master. He only needs to be given instructions for the task at hand, and then he can follow them without any further relationship to the master.

  Many Christians strive to live in accordance with the moral guidelines expressed in the Bible (or at least their understanding of those guidelines within their own Christian cultural context). It is easy to fall into the pattern of getting to know what the book says and then following the instructions. But, carried to the extreme, the book can become an idol that hinders relationship with the Father.

- A son follows the Father. A son's interests will be aligned with the Father's purpose. It is not enough for him to hear instructions and then run off and do them. He would much rather do things together with his Father. The son will long to understand what motivates the Father, to hear his heartbeat, and to reproduce his nature.

  Jesus was frequently accused of breaking the Law. But he said that he never did anything apart from

---

34 See Romans 6:4-7 and Colossians 2:11-15

his Father.[35] In the eyes of the servant-oriented pharisees, Jesus was a law-breaker. But in the eyes of his Father he was a pleasing Son. It is a mistake to interpret the grace of God as a license to do whatever we want.[36] A son is free from the bondage of the rules through his commitment to living in accordance with these things: bringing pleasure to his father and strengthening the relationship between father and son.

Interaction

- A servant interacts within a framework of hierarchy. In practice, he has no peers – only people whose instructions he is expected to follow and (perhaps) people whom he expects to follow his instructions.

  The servant mentality results in a feeling of insecurity when there are not clearly defined lines of control and structural authority, because servanthood is rooted in rules and performance. There is a tendency to push all interpersonal relationships into a hierarchical framework, in the family, in the workplace, and especially in the church.

- A son interacts relationally. A son looks upon everyone they relate to as someone to be honored. A person walking in sonship operates primarily in a framework of being part of a team. The accomplishments of the team are a fruit of the team's successful interaction, rather than a goal in itself.

---

35 John 5:19, 30
36 Such an attitude is really a veiled expression of servanthood

A sonship mentality seeks to lift up others and see them excel, because a son has no need to demonstrate his own value. A son's interaction with the people around him focuses on enhancing the relationship, because the health of the relationship affects the identity, motivation and destiny of everyone whom the relationship touches.

Motivation

- A servant is largely motivated by pain-avoidance. He will typically choose the path of least resistance, and tend to look no farther than the next situation to be tackled.

It is easy to succumb to the illusion that, since you have been saved by grace at no cost to yourself, then it ought to be possible to walk effortlessly into the fulness of life in Christ. With such a line of thinking you might tend to interpret any hindrance or attack of the enemy as a reason to turn aside. The result is a lack of maturity and strength.

- A son is motivated by a higher goal; something at a distance but with such value that it is worth the cost of getting there.

It was the joy set before him that motivated Jesus to endure the Cross.[37] It was the value of the goal that made enduring the pain to achieve that goal worthwhile.

---

37 Hebrews 12:1-3

Destiny

- A servant looks for his master to tell him what to do. The servant's purpose and calling are determined by his master in order to meet the master's needs.

  There are Christians who are looking to discern the will of God for their life. They figure that God has some master plan where they are a piece in the puzzle. They just need to somehow figure out which piece they are and get themselves put into the right place. For some reason, it is not uncommon to think that their place in the puzzle is something very different from what they would choose for themselves, as if the will of God were a manipulative and arbitrary thing.

- A son dreams together with his father. A son understands that he has a heritage which has planted something in him. The discovery of these dreams, calling and destiny is an adventure that father and son can explore in fellowship.

  Father God created each of us with a unique personality, a glorious destiny and a precious birthright. These things are interrelated, such that our personal preferences, giftings, interests and dreams equip us for the destiny and birthright that are ours to claim. The Father watches with great anticipation to see how the things he has planted in us will grow and blossom. And they will grow best under the nurture of a close relationship between Father and son.

Faith and trust

- A servant sees his master primarily through the lens of information and consequences. His perspective is framed by his ability to wrap his mind around the actions of his master.

  Some believers feel a need to understand what God is doing in order to trust that it is really God. But this need is really a form of control, which is the opposite of faith. The "faith" that says "I won't trust what I don't understand" is not faith at all. In the Kingdom of Heaven, understanding comes not through knowledge but through trusting and following.[38]

- A son accepts what his father is doing because he trusts his father. His first reaction will be one of joyous wonder, whether he understands what is going on or not.

  Of course, this kind of trust can be broken (and perhaps do horrible damage) if a father abuses his child's trust. But Father God is completely good and always trustworthy. He has never let you down,[39] and he will never do so.

When Jesus talked about the difference between servanthood and friendship[40] (John 15), it was in the context of fruitfulness. He said that just as a branch can

---

38 See Proverbs 3:5-6
39 An in-depth look at the problem of pain is beyond the scope of this book. However, if you feel that God has let you down I encourage you to approach the Father in childlike trust and ask him to show you where he was and what he was doing when that thing happened. I believe he will reveal himself as trustworthy.
40 In this context, friendship and sonship are very much the same thing.

only bear fruit when it is attached to the vine, so will our fruitfulness be a consequence of a close relationship to him. Not only that, but he went on to say that we could ask whatever we wish and that our fruitfulness would bring glory to the Father! One of the discoveries I have made in recent years is that I tend to be more fruitful when I am simply living a life of relationship to the Father than when I am trying (through my own efforts) to produce fruit for his Kingdom.

The veil of servanthood

This concept of sonship/friendship was a huge offense to the Jewish leaders of Jesus' time, and it remains so to this day. Paul refers to this hindrance as the veil which hid the glory of God from the listeners, and which has not been taken away.[41]

It was the Israelites themselves who asked for the veil. God's intention and invitation was for Israel to be a kingdom of priests[42] – which meant that the door was open for every person to have a direct relationship to God. However, when God spoke from the mountain to this group of newly-delivered slaves, they were terrified by the enormity of his voice and his being. So they cried out for Moses to stand between them and God.[43] They wanted Moses to listen to God and report to them and tell them what to do. In so doing, they asked for something less than the direct relationship with God that was being offered to them. In other words, they asked to stay in a servant relationship.

---

41 2 Corinthians 3:13-15
42 Exodus 19:6
43 Exodus 20:18-19

Later, came the discovery that, after he had been in the presence of God, the face of Moses shone with the glory of God. In fact, it shone so much that the people were filled with fear and could hardly stand to look at Moses. So they asked him to cover his face with a veil, at least until the glory faded.[44] Little did they know that the consequence of their request was that their ability to relate to God in the way he desired for them became more or less paralyzed.

The religious leaders of Jesus' day were blinded by this veil. As a prophetic act, Jesus gave sight to a man born blind. He wanted to demonstrate that the time for removing the veil was at hand. But the religious leaders chose rather to cling to their servant-oriented understanding of God's ways.[45]

When Jesus died on the Cross, the veil in the temple was torn in two from top to bottom,[46] opening the way (for all who were looking to see the invitation) to move from a life of servanthood to a position of sonship. Even so, most of the Jews in Jerusalem missed out on the invitation, especially those who professed to be experts in knowing the ways of God. In the following years, until Jerusalem was destroyed, perhaps as many as half of the Jews there came to a saving belief in Jesus. Even so, many of them clung fast to their servant-oriented understanding of their relationship to God.[47]

How did they manage to miss out? I suspect that a major factor is due to a mistaken understanding of the position of Moses in the history of Israel. Moses is referred to as

---

44 Exodus 34:29-35
45 John 9:28-29
46 Matthew 27:51
47 Acts 21:20-21

the servant of God,[48] which is less than the destiny to which God has called his people.

Please don't misunderstand me here. Moses has a unique position in history as a man who spoke with God face to face. There is no doubt that he understood his position of sonship, he who time after time argued with God and even convinced God to change his mind. But Moses' calling was to transform a group of miserable slaves into a glorious nation that could become a resting place for the glory of God. This was a good thing, but it was only part of an even greater calling on this people chosen by God.

Although Moses was a great leader, he was not the patriarch of this people. To get to the roots of the calling, we need to go back to the first patriarch who was called out: Abraham, the friend of God.[49] The calling of Abraham is all about blessing:

> "I will make you into a great nation, and I will bless you; I will make your name great, and you will be a blessing. I will bless those who bless you, and whoever curses you I will curse; and all peoples on Earth will be blessed through you." (Genesis 12:2-3)

This is a sonship calling. The calling was not deserved, but rather freely offered by God's sovereign choice; it does not depend on the performance of those who are called; and it has a destiny that rests firmly on the purposes of God: that all peoples on Earth will be blessed.

The Law of Moses, though completely the word of God, was yet an incomplete revelation of the nature of God. It

---

48 1 Chronicles 6:49, 2 Chronicles 24:9, Nehemiah 10:29, Daniel 9:11
49 2 Chronicles 20:7, Isaiah 41:8, James 2:23

was an important part of transforming a nation of slaves to a people for God's own possession. And yet, it had its limitations because its initial audience was, in fact, a people who knew nothing but servanthood. For example, the Law permitted divorce, even though divorce is inconsistent with the nature of God. Jesus said that the reason for this inconsistency was the hardness of their hearts.[50] In other words, the Law was, at least to some degree, tailored to the condition of the people who received the Law.

The purpose of the Law was not so much to portray the nature or will of God as it was to demonstrate the people's need for a savior.[51] The requirements of the Law give an indication of how unreachable holiness is, and how impossible it is to walk in holiness through one's own strength. The underlying message is: You can't do this on your own, so come to me.

And yet, this not quite perfect Law is still a good thing. A very good thing in the eyes of most Jews, then and today. Herein lies the challenge, and perhaps also the key. Being a servant of God, in the order of Moses, is actually a pretty good life. But at the same time, it restricts the servants from seeing that they are rather invited to be friends of God in the order of Abraham. I wonder if this might be a key to opening an understanding of the Gospel to the Jewish people – not so much a focus only on believing in Jesus as the Messiah as also a focus on the invitation to look beyond service in accordance with the Law to the blessing of Abraham's call as portrayed by Jesus the Son.

---

50   Matthew 19:8
51   Romans 3:20

Food for thought

In what ways are you relating to the Lord as a servant rather than as a son or daughter? Is pain-avoidance a factor in the decisions you make? Are there good things that you allow to stand in the way of your entering into the destiny that God has made available to you?

In what ways do images (or imaginations) of your human father influence and distort your ability to see the nature of Father God? What is the truth about his nature?

Home

When Abraham was living in the land of Harran, the Lord called him to depart from his home and family. This call carried a great blessing but it also carried an unknown destination.

> *By faith Abraham, when called to go to a place he would later receive as his inheritance, obeyed and went, even though he did not know where he was going. By faith he made his home in the promised land like a stranger in a foreign country; he lived in tents, as did Isaac and Jacob, who were heirs with him of the same promise. For he was looking forward to the city with foundations, whose architect and builder is God.*
>
> *All these people were still living by faith when they died. They did not receive the things promised; they only saw them and welcomed them from a distance, admitting that they were foreigners and strangers on Earth. People who say such things show that they are looking for a country of their own. If they had been thinking of the country they*

> had left, they would have had opportunity to return. Instead, they were longing for a better country—a heavenly one. Therefore God is not ashamed to be called their God, for he has prepared a city for them. (Hebrews 11:8-10, 13-16)

In other words, the Lord invited Abraham on a journey to something that was out of reach. But something about the invitation was so appealing that Abraham went for it. The writer of Hebrews calls it a better country, a city with foundations. In Revelation 21, John refers to it as the Holy City, the new Jerusalem, prepared as a bride for her husband, the dwelling place of God among the people. All of this points to a true home.

I don't know what comes to your mind when you hear the word home. Perhaps you think of the house where you sleep at night. Or perhaps you think of the place where you spent your formative years. For me, the word home implies identity, safety, belonging and rest.

Before the creation of this world, the Lord existed in a fellowship of Father, Son and Spirit. We call this the Trinity or the Triune God; the idea being that there is one God in three Persons. The first century believers referred to this relationship as a dance:[52] Father, Son and Spirit moving in step with one another in an atmosphere of love and unity.

When mankind was created in the image of God, we were created to take part in this dance. Each of us is created with an innate calling and longing to be "at home" in the center of the dance. That is where we belong. It is where we were designed to find our identity, safety and rest.

---

52 The Greek term perichoresis (circle-dance) was used by early theologians to describe the dynamic of the Trinity.

Unfortunately, when sin entered the world, the ability of the human race to see God (as he truly is) died. Instead, we see him through the distorted perspective of things like fear, shame and inadequacy. It is really hard to stay in step with a dance partner that you can't see. Consequently, we find ourselves outside of the dance – away from our true home.

A person in this state, being on the outside – away from home and away from the Father, is in essence an orphan. Since they do not have the experience of being cared for and protected by a father, they feel as though they need to do it all themselves. No one is going to tell them what to do, they are going to control their own life and circumstances. Once this pattern establishes itself, it becomes very difficult to trust other people, especially people in authority. The constant need to insure their own provision and safety means that they can not rest and are never really at peace.

This orphan state[53] stands in opposition to our invitation to come home to God the Father. But, I believe there is a key to breaking out of this fatherlessness. When the God the Son was born into this world, the angels sang peace on Earth. And Jesus said, "Blessed are the peacemakers, for they will be called children of God."[54] There is a connection between peace and sonship.

Rather than laboring to shape our circumstances so that we might feel safe, we can experience true peace. It involves trusting the Prince of Peace, and learning to think as he does. It involves acting on behalf of others

---

53 Or rather, orphan spirit. The original "orphan" was Lucifer, whose ambition was to replace the Father with himself. See Isaiah 14:12-14
54 Matthew 5:9

rather than defending ourselves. Cultivating the heart of a peacemaker breaks the orphan pattern and opens the pathway home.

When the prodigal son came to his senses, he thought of home. He knew he did not deserve to be welcomed home, but that longing for identity, safety and rest tugged hard at him. In his heart, he knew where he belonged, even if the circumstances were telling him that he did not belong. Like Abraham, he set out without knowing what would meet him.

To his great surprise, his father welcomed him home as a son. And to make sure that he understood it, his father clothed him as a son who belonged there. He probably didn't feel like he had been a son to his father, so this may have been difficult for him to receive. But the message is very clear: Father God greatly desires to be a father to his children, those who walk closely with him, those who faithfully serve him and also those who after having been lost begin to take feeble steps toward him.

Sonship is a two-way street. Mostly, we have looked at sonship from the perspective of having a father. Equally important is being a son. Think of the pain and loss this father has experienced through the years that he invested in two young men whose hearts were not set on being sons to their father.

Jesus said that he only did what he saw his Father doing, that he only spoke the words that his Father spoke, and that he delighted to do the will of his Father. That is being a son. Those are the steps of the dance. This is home.

Food for thought

Imagine yourself in the midst of the dance. What does that look like to you? How does it make you feel? How do you learn the steps of the dance? What does the dance show you about the King and his Kingdom?

Extravagant

As we saw in the previous chapter, the father did not hold back his resources when it came to bringing life to his children. Nothing would stand in the way of him expressing his love. We can see this from another angle in the parable of the sower. Here's the parable and Jesus' explanation of it, as recorded by Mark:

> Listen! A farmer went out to sow his seed. As he was scattering the seed, some fell along the path, and the birds came and ate it up. Some fell on rocky places, where it did not have much soil. It sprang up quickly, because the soil was shallow. But when the sun came up, the plants were scorched, and they withered because they had no root. Other seed fell among thorns, which grew up and choked the plants, so that they did not bear grain. Still other seed fell on good soil. It came up, grew and produced a crop, some multiplying thirty, some sixty, some a hundred times. (Mark 4:3-8)

> Then Jesus said to them, "Don't you understand this parable? How then will you understand any parable? The farmer sows the word. Some people are like seed along the path, where the word is sown. As soon as they hear it, Satan comes and takes away the word that was sown in them. Others, like seed sown on rocky places, hear the word and at once receive it with joy. But since they have no root, they last only a short time. When trouble or persecution comes because of the word,

they quickly fall away. Still others, like seed sown among thorns, hear the word; but the worries of this life, the deceitfulness of wealth and the desires for other things come in and choke the word, making it unfruitful. Others, like seed sown on good soil, hear the word, accept it, and produce a crop—some thirty, some sixty, some a hundred times what was sown." (Mark 4:13-20)

This parable and its explanation show how the events of a parable are used to illustrate spiritual truths or principles. For example, just as a bird, whose purposes are opposed to the will of the sower, takes away the seed sown on unreceptive soil, so also the enemy of God takes away the word of God when it falls on unreceptive ears.

Since Jesus has explained the central symbolism of the parable, I will not presume to expand so much on that. But there are still a few aspects of the story that are worth a closer examination.

Extravagance

First, the sower doesn't seem to have been too careful about where the seed was sown. If I were a farmer with a limited amount of seed, then I would probably make an effort to be sure that as much of the seed as possible was sown on good soil. But that doesn't seem to have been an issue in this story.

Perhaps the reason is that the supply of seed (the word of God) is unlimited. Perhaps it is because the soil quality is not evident until later, so that the potential to be good soil was reason enough for seed to be sown on it. Perhaps it is simply because the sower is extravagant.

Although God may be extravagant with his word, he is not wasteful. For his word does not go out without achieving the purpose for which it was sent.[55] And the purposes of God spring out from his unlimited and generous nature; they are neither stingy nor impoverished.

The word of God is a gift, freely given to all who would receive it. And the purpose of a gift lies entirely in the giver. A gift becomes no less a gift by my failure or refusal to receive the gift. If I must do or achieve something (such as being good soil) in order to receive a gift, then it is no longer a gift but rather some form of compensation for my actions.

Father God, in his wisdom, extravagantly scatters his word abroad. The word falls on all kinds of people, and by the receptiveness of their hearts (soil) the word may or may not bear fruit. It is the very fact that each person is free to choose whether or not to be receptive that makes the good soil so valuable. The desire of God's heart is that everyone would choose to be receptive to his word. But it is the freely chosen embracing of his word that most touches his heart.

This boundless generosity is a natural consequence of God's loving nature. From the simple act of sending rain on the righteous and the unrighteous[56] to the sacrifice of his beloved son, the works of Father God are extravagant.

---

55   Isaiah 55:10-11
56   Matthew 5:45

Food for thought

In what ways does the extravagant nature of Father God influence your daily life? Do you expect goodness? Do you fear what might go wrong? Do you view the goodness of God as something you need to earn or perform well enough to deserve? Is your perspective true to his nature?

To what extent is the extravagance of Father God reflected in your daily life? Are you viewed as generous? Do you place expectations on how people should respond to your kindness?

Potential

For God's gifts and his call are irrevocable. (Romans 11:29)

Another aspect of God's extravagance is that he calls imperfect people to walk with him. The biblical record is full of people who have been called and anointed by God. Pretty much all of them failed in some point, and far too many failed completely. But that didn't stop God from calling. And, in fact, he calls far more people today[57] than the chosen few who were called in the Old Testament age.

Are you able to catch a glimpse of the nature of the Father here? In his wisdom he chooses to risk giving gifts and calling to a person based only on the *potential* for what they might achieve! Even though he knows the end from the beginning, and knows the failures that will come, he still chooses to take the risk!

I find it fascinating, and somewhat incomprehensible. The God who created the universe places a higher value

---

57 Joel 3:1

on potential than on avoiding risk. He is The Rock,[58] unmovable, unshakable, unassailable, completely secure in his position as I AM. So, in a sense, there is no risk. He sees potential, and his joy is to see that potential come to fruition.

Food for thought

Do you see the potential in the people with whom you interact? Do you give people the freedom to fail, or do you try to control their circumstances in order to prevent them from making bad choices? Are you able to trust Father with managing your risk?

Soil

The sower scatters seed. The seed is the word of God. Or as Matthew put it, the seed is the message about the Kingdom. This message is far more encompassing than just the gospel of salvation. If we restrict our understanding of his message to only that part of the word of God that is about getting people through the door of salvation, then we have touched only the shore of a vast and deep ocean.

In the very beginning, God spoke and his word created the world. And the creation continues to reflect the word and nature of God even to this day.[59] The Bible gives us a clear and objective record of the word of God. And that record shows that God speaks through prophets, through visions, through dreams, and a myriad of other ways.

---

58 Deuteronomy 23:3-4
59 Romans 1:20

All of this revelation is being extravagantly sown. But, if we are looking for no more than the gospel of salvation then we will be like the path or the stony ground in relation to the bulk of the message.

What can we do to be like good soil for all the word of God? The key is to abide in him, to have eyes fixed firmly on the things above and a heart that is in alignment with his heart. Jesus said, "I no longer call you servants, because a servant does not know his master's business. Instead, I have called you friends, for everything that I learned from my Father I have made known to you."[60] In other words, by relating to the Lord as a friend you will be more fruitful soil than by relating to him as a servant.

A servant sees the word of his master as instructions to be carried out and rules to be followed. He has no vested interest in what lies on his master's heart, he just wants to meet his obligations and be done with it. This perspective puts limitations on his ability to receive the word. The word becomes a rule book or an instruction manual. Words that touch on love, acceptance, romance, freedom, friendship, joy, and the like, will not so easily take root in such soil.

A friend, however, is able to receive and embrace a much wider scale of communication. Reading the Bible as a friend is mostly about reading to understand the nature and the heart of the One who is the source of the words therein. The commands and instructions found there are not so much rules to obey as they are indicators of how the Lord thinks and what he values. In this context, obedience is the fruit of a desire to please a friend rather than an attempt to be acceptable to a master.

---

60   John 15:15

A friend shares the thoughts of his heart with his friend. The word that is sown on good soil is not restricted to only the written Word of the Bible, but also encompasses all of the ways that a person can communicate with their friend.[61] Dreams, visions, thoughts, impressions, words of knowledge or wisdom are all examples of ways that the Lord uses to share his heart with his friends. Such communication is personal, expressly suited to fit the nature of the person who is walking in friendship with his or her Lord. And it is a communication that encourages closer friendship. Often, the Lord speaks in a manner that leaves us with questions that can only be answered by seeking more of him. For, "apart from me you can do nothing."[62]

As we walk more closely in friendship, we discover that much of the message of the Kingdom is about friendship with a Good Father and what that means in practice. This friendship encompasses our royal position as sons and daughters of the King. It grows as we step into freedom from the bondage that the enemy would place on us. And, among other things, it gives us access to the gifts of Heaven by which we can demonstrate the goodness of God and bring that freedom to people around us.

Consider what you hear

It is also wise to consider the company you keep. History is filled with examples of people who began well, but finished poorly. Among these are Solomon and Hezekiah,

---

61 Even so, the Lord communicates consistently. No dream, vision or prophecy will be inconsistent with his written Word, although there may be times that we need to seek his heart more clearly to understand how things fit together.

62 John 15:5b

kings of Israel who began their reign with wisdom and favor before God and men, whose kingdoms were known for peace and plenty, but whose final days were tarnished by a failure to walk closely with the God they had worshiped so faithfully in the beginning. In Solomon's case it was the deceitfulness of a wealth of foreign wives that led him to unfaithfulness.[63] In the case of Hezekiah, his faithfulness transformed into pride, especially after envoys from the king of Babylon came to honor (or flatter) him.[64] Another was King Joash, who followed the Lord as long as the priest Jehoiada (who had been as a father to Joash) lived, but after his death gave ear to ungodly counsel and turned from the Lord.[65]

Each of these kings allowed people around them to gain such influence in their lives that their friendship with the Lord became tarnished. What had once been good and productive soil became cluttered with undesirable growth.

I call this the principle of "garbage in, garbage out." If you fill your mind with garbage, then the outcome is going to stink. Who or what you allow to bring counsel to your ears will, in the end, influence the direction of your life. Obviously, the friends and role models that you choose will have their impact. Even more so, the inputs from media that you allow to flood your mind can contribute to the growth of thorns that will choke the message of the Kingdom.

Jesus said:

---

63   1 Kings 11:1-6
64   2 Chronicles 32:25
65   2 Chronicles 24:17-18

> *"Consider carefully what you hear," he continued. "With the measure you use, it will be measured to you—and even more. Whoever has will be given more; whoever does not have, even what they have will be taken from them." (Mark 4:24-25)*

This is a double-edged sword. If our response to God's revelation to us, be it through his written word or through his many other forms of communication, is doubt or skepticism then we may find that his stream of revelation to us dries up. And if we allow the measure of other inputs in our life to increase then they may eventually become a flood in which we drown.

We are called to be ambassadors for Christ and to disciple nations.[66] However, this calling is not fulfilled by appointing ourselves as guardians of the truth. The tendency to look at everything with an eye for finding something wrong will poison the soil.

> *Do not speak against one another, brethren. He who speaks against a brother, or judges his brother, speaks against the law, and judges the law; but if you judge the law, you are not a doer of the law, but a judge of it. (James 4:11 NASB)*

I am frequently saddened by Christian voices that seem to feel a calling to criticize or condemn anyone or anything they might find to be theologically out of line. They can be quick to pronounce heresy, without necessarily looking with a desire to understand the heart of the issue at hand. That kind of hardness does not make for soil that is easily plowed.[67]

---

66 2 Corinthians 5:20 and Matthew 28:19
67 Of course, there are central tenets of the faith (such as the deity of Christ, the victory of the Cross, etc) that must not be

Rather, our calling is to be good soil that drinks deeply of the revelation that rains upon us.[68] Among the key characteristics of God's nature are love, freedom and holiness – and these three are not in conflict with each other. So why would we expect the word to be primarily restrictive in nature? Something is wrong if our view of the holiness of God is framed by the idea that everything is forbidden except for what his word specifically allows.

For example, I have heard of believers who have excluded the use of musical instruments from their practice of worship. Their conclusion is that since musical instruments are not specifically mentioned in the context of worship[69] in the new testament, then they should not be used in worship. Such logic appears to me to be based on a misunderstanding of the holiness of God, one that fails to see his holiness in light of his nature of love and freedom. This kind of restrictive perspective makes for unfruitful soil.

Paul instructed the Thessalonians to look carefully at things and to keep the good stuff.[70] In other words, we should not reject everything a person says just because

> compromised. But most of the theological disputes that arise are not around the central issues. Paul's admonition in Romans 16:17 which might be interpreted as a call to reject the "heretics" specifically speaks about people who cause division (which might just be you or me if we are not careful) and needs to be practiced in the light of what Paul wrote in chapter 14: That our behavior needs to primarily be framed around honoring other believers who might not see everything the way we do.

68 Hebrews 6:7-8
69 At least not in English. The Norwegian translation of Colossians 3:16 says "sing and play with a glad heart," which implies the use of instruments.
70 1 Thessalonians 5:19-22

we find disagreeable some aspect of what they said or how they said it.[71] Good soil is able to receive fertilizer (which might just smell like manure) and transform it into the nutrients that foster fruitfulness.

On the other hand, we are not called to be sewers. Which is why Jesus said, "Consider carefully what you hear." It is just as wrong to flood your mind with sewage on the chance that an occasional useful tidbit might float by as it is to reject mostly good inputs out of fear that you might actually hear something that doesn't fit your theology.

I am not saying that you must never listen to a secular song or that you must trash your TV or close your facebook account. But do you give attention to the stream of thoughts that flows into your mind from the media that surround you? More often than one might realize, songs, films and even news broadcasts are scripted with the intent to make a statement and to influence our point of view. In other words, the seeds of thorns are constantly being sown in our direction; what matters is whether or not we allow them to take root. And thorns have a tendency to take root anywhere you are not vigilant about preventing their growth.

> *"Who among us can live with the consuming fire? Who among us can live with continual burning?" He who walks righteously and speaks with sincerity, he who rejects unjust gain and shakes his hands so that they hold no bribe; he who stops his ears from hearing about bloodshed and shuts his eyes from looking upon evil; he will dwell on*

---

71 Neither should we condemn or curse any person, regardless of how wrong some or all of what they say or do may be. See James 3:9-10 and Romans 14:4

> *the heights, his refuge will be the impregnable rock; his bread will be given him, his water will be sure. Your eyes will see the King in His beauty; they will behold a far-distant land. (Isaiah 33:14b-17 NASB)*

This passage from Isaiah is very clear, and has profound implications for our taste in film, music, games and more. The person who fills their mind with dishonesty, bloodshed and evil will not be able to stand before the presence of our God (who is a consuming fire). But the one who avoids these things will see the King and his Kingdom.

What you should or shouldn't hear is individual. Some people are called to speak into secular environments with an authority that comes from knowing and participating in the dialogue at hand. Others are called to walk in a purity of heart that must not be stained by unnecessary exposure to the ways of this world. The leading of the Holy Spirit is essential here: He will gladly counsel you as you consider carefully what you hear, and lead you to open the healthy doors and close the unhealthy ones.

> *"Above all else, guard your heart, for everything you do flows from it." (Proverbs 4:23)*

Food for thought

What do you think about Father God wanting to be friends with you? Do you find it easier to follow rules than to develop friendship? Are you receptive to hearing the Lord speak in new ways?

What is the stream of inputs to your thoughts like? Are you conscious of how these inputs may try to form your opinions? Are wise and godly voices the ones that are influential in your life?

Has the Holy Spirit prompted you to consider the value of any films, video games, news channels or whatever might be a part of your daily life?

Thorns

You might have noticed that the seed was sown on three different types of soil: hard soil, soil without depth, and good soil. However, there were two different outcomes for the seed sown on good soil: Abundance or lack of fruitfulness and maturity. And that difference was a result of the absence or presence of thorns.

Jesus said that the thorns represent the worries of this life, the deceitfulness of wealth and the desires for other things. He also said that these things can choke the word, thereby preventing fruitfulness and maturity. Did you notice that the thorns are attitudes? It is the *worries* of this life and the *deceitfulness* of wealth, rather than this life or wealth in itself, that chokes the word.

As I see it, there are two ways that thorns can choke the word: there are the thorns which are already in place when the word is sown, and there are the thorns which are allowed to take root in competition with the word that has already been sown. But in both cases, the soil is good. This represents a challenge facing everyone who seeks the Kingdom, because thorns grow where there is lack of discipline in maintaining a receptive environment for the message of the Kingdom. You can't just clear out the thorns once and assume that they will stay away.

> *The way of the sluggard is blocked with thorns, but the path of the upright is a highway. (Proverbs 15:9)*

Worries of this life

What, then, are the worries of this life? They have to do with getting our everyday needs met, from such basic needs as food, clothing and shelter to meeting the stress and expectations of daily life. These are not bad things, and it is not wrong to carry out the business of daily life. But if we allow the *worries* of these things to consume us, then they will choke the message of the Kingdom.

> *Do not be anxious about anything, but in every situation, by prayer and petition, with thanksgiving, present your requests to God. And the peace of God, which transcends all understanding, will guard your hearts and your minds in Christ Jesus. (Philippians 4:6-7)*

Worry is a misdirected form of meditation. It focuses the thoughts on what could go wrong, on what is lacking, or on what doesn't work. It is fear-based rather than faith-based. Worry invalidates trust, it exhausts the worrier's strength and it strangles thankfulness. Worry is a symptom of the need to control one's circumstances; which is the opposite of faith.

Do you see how worry can choke the message of a generous and loving Father who is King over a Kingdom with abundant resources? It is difficult for the worrier to receive a message about a Father who wants his children to succeed and prosper, who wants to give them good gifts, and who wants them to live joyously. In the end, worry says that our extravagant Father does not exist.

What can be done? Here is a good antidote for worry:

> *Finally, brethren, whatever is true, whatever is honorable, whatever is right, whatever is pure, whatever is lovely, whatever is of good repute, if there is any excellence or if anything worthy of praise, let your mind dwell on these things. (Philippians 4:8 NASB)*

Deceitfulness of wealth

The deceitfulness of wealth is a somewhat thornier issue. It is the very fact that wealth can deceitfully sneak its way into choking the message sown on good soil, that calls us to diligence.

It is not having wealth that is the problem, but rather if wealth has us. Wealth is not evil in itself. But even the beautiful rose has thorns. The challenge with wealth is to not be damaged by its thorns.

Wealth has a tendency to replace God as a source of security. This doesn't happen suddenly, but as a series of small steps that encroach on our lives just as weeds and brambles encroach on a garden. The person who has nothing will find it easy to look to God as their provider. But the more God provides, the easier it becomes to look more at the provision than at the provider. Sometimes, the Lord holds wealth from us to protect us from its deceitfulness.

What can be done? I believe that generosity and thankfulness are useful tools for weeding the thorns out of the garden of life. The early Christians did not consider their wealth as their own, but they shared freely with one another.[72] It wasn't that they all sold everything and lived communally. But they had a lifestyle of continuously making resources available so that their fellowship would flourish; and yet always with an ear to the Lord's leadership.

The Old Testament practice of tithing was, among other things, designed to help counteract the deceitfulness of wealth.

> *Be sure to set aside a tenth of all that your fields produce each year. Eat the tithe of your grain, new wine and olive oil, and the firstborn of your herds and flocks in the presence of the Lord your God at the place he will choose as a dwelling for his Name, so that you may learn to revere the Lord your God always. But if that place is too distant and you have been blessed by the Lord your God and cannot carry your tithe (because the place where the Lord will choose to put his Name is so far away), then exchange your tithe for silver, and take the silver with you and go to the place the Lord your God will choose. Use the silver to buy whatever you like: cattle, sheep, wine or other fermented drink, or anything you wish. Then you and your household shall eat there in the presence of the Lord your God and rejoice. (Deuteronomy 14:22-26)*

As you can see here, the purpose of this tithe was to finance a party in the presence of the Lord. The purpose of this wealth was so that worshiping the Lord in his presence would be a pleasurable thing, that the

---

72 Acts 4:32

worshipers would joyfully eat and drink and be satisfied in fellowship with their God. *And* that this fellowship and party atmosphere would welcome and share with the poor and disadvantaged people (foreigners, fatherless, widows, etc) in the community.[73]

It appears that this practice of sharing with the disadvantaged had a central position in the life and practice of the early church. The church in Jerusalem had a daily distribution of food[74] (apparently for those who were unable to care for themselves), and Paul instructed Timothy about the care of widows, through family, friendships and the congregation.[75] This is the kind of lifestyle that helps keep the thorns out of the garden.

As we saw in the three parables of something that was lost, the Father likes to party. It only makes sense that when our Father the King throws a party, he does so extravagantly.

Food for thought

How much time and energy do you spend thinking about what might go wrong? Do you really trust the Lord, even when you don't see the solution?

Why do you have the wealth that you have? Are you thankful for what you have been given or discouraged/disappointed by what you lack? Is rejoicing in fellowship with the Father and his people a priority?

---

73 Deuteronomy 14:27-29
74 Acts 6:1
75 1 Timothy 5:3-16

Unshakable

As we saw from the parable of the sower, the seed was sown extravagantly. In Matthew's record, Jesus followed up with another parable that looked at this extravagance from another angle.

> *The Kingdom of Heaven is like a man who sowed good seed in his field. But while everyone was sleeping, his enemy came and sowed weeds among the wheat, and went away. When the wheat sprouted and formed heads, then the weeds also appeared. The owner's servants came to him and said, "Sir, didn't you sow good seed in your field? Where then did the weeds come from?"*
>
> *"An enemy did this," he replied.*
>
> *The servants asked him, "Do you want us to go and pull them up?"*
>
> *"No," he answered, "because while you are pulling the weeds, you may uproot the wheat with them. Let both grow together until the harvest. At that time I will tell the harvesters: First collect the weeds and tie them in bundles to be burned; then gather the wheat and bring it into my barn." (Matthew 13:24-30)*

And the explanation:

> *The one who sowed the good seed is the Son of Man. The field is the world, and the good seed stands for the people of the Kingdom. The weeds are the people of the evil one, and the enemy who*

> *sows them is the devil. The harvest is the end of the age, and the harvesters are angels. As the weeds are pulled up and burned in the fire, so it will be at the end of the age. The Son of Man will send out his angels, and they will weed out of his Kingdom everything that causes sin and all who do evil. They will throw them into the blazing furnace, where there will be weeping and gnashing of teeth. Then the righteous will shine like the sun in the Kingdom of their Father. (Matthew 13:37-43)*

As Jesus explained, this parable illustrates how the harvest at the end of the age will sweep away the weeds and bring about a glorious revelation of the Kingdom of God.

Holding the course

What captures my attention in this parable is the unshakableness (if that is a valid word) of the sower. When he saw the results of his enemy's sneak attack, he didn't panic, worry, or allow himself to be thrown off course by these circumstances.

Apparently, the enemy's motivation was to mess up the sower's crop in order to reduce its value or to increase the sower's expenses, so that the sower would suffer loss. We might speculate as to how the enemy figured this loss would manifest itself:

- If the weeds were removed when they first became evident, then there would be the extra labor expense of the weeding process, in addition to the potential loss of damaged wheat during the weeding.

- If the weeds were allowed to grow, they might limit the growth of the wheat, by stealing space, soil, nutrients, and water.
- If the weeds were mixed together with the wheat at the harvest, then the quality of the crop would be compromised, or even destroyed.

In other words, the enemy's attack was rooted in the enemy's hatred toward the sower. But the attack was actually rather petty; an act of bitterness and spite. Apparently, the enemy didn't have the resources or the courage to attack the sower directly,[76] so instead he resorted in the darkness of night to what he thought (within his means) might hurt the sower.

The sower's response to this attack was to not allow the actions of his enemy to influence his thinking. The potential loss scenarios were the result of thought patterns based on lies:

- The enemy can hurt me.
- There aren't enough resources to go around.
- The weeds will contaminate the wheat.

Rather than taking fear-based action, the sower chose to hold out until the harvest, secure in the knowledge that this work of his enemy would not diminish his goals. In essence, he was saying, "I refuse to let the enemy dictate the course of my life." The result is a harvest that shines like the sun in the Kingdom of the Father.

---

[76] Which is true about the devil today: Having been disarmed by the Cross, his ability to attack is limited to what he can deceive us into believing he can do.

Neither did the sower allow himself to be enticed into mounting a counter-attack against his enemy. Another of the devil's lies is that he is an enemy who is actually powerful enough to be worth attacking. The enemy would like us to do battle with him on his terms. But the strength of this Kingdom is found when standing firm in our position, seated in heavenly places in Christ Jesus[77].

In my opinion, it was the enemy who ended up suffering loss. His attack on the sower failed completely to impose any loss on the sower, and all of the efforts of the enemy came to nothing.

However, if the sower had let himself be deceived by the lies of his enemy; if he had let himself be driven to action by fear of the weeds or what they might do, then he most certainly would have suffered loss. The enemy is actually totally powerless[78] except when we give him power over us by believing his lies.

These principles apply to the attacks which our enemy, the devil, may throw at us in our daily lives. It is the shield of faith[79] that nullifies these attacks. And faith is the assurance of things hoped for.[80] Our steadfast confidence in the goodness and unshakableness of our loving Father disarms and neutralizes any attack of the enemy.

These principles also apply to the story of human history. When God the Father planted his children in the Garden of Eden, an enemy came in the form of a serpent and through his deception the human race became weeds.

---

77 See Ephesians 6:11 and 2:6
78 See Colossians 2:15
79 Ephesians 6:16
80 Hebrews 11:1 NASB

But God is not taken by surprise. In essence, he looked at the situation and said, "I've got it covered. For the Lamb who was slain from the foundation of the world[81] has defeated the enemy. And at the end of the age I will sort it all out. There will be no loss."

Food for thought

In what ways does the enemy manage to gain influence in your life? What are the lies that give the enemy access to you? What truths about Father God and his Kingdom will disperse those lies? Do you experience Father God as a rock that can not be shaken?

The harvest

Jesus said that the weeds are the people of the evil one. He also said that the weeds represent two things: everything that causes sin and all who do evil.

Note that he says all who *do* evil, rather than all who have done evil. If being a person of the evil one is defined by having done evil, then there would be no people of the Kingdom. For all have sinned and fall short of the glory of God.[82] But the people of the evil one are those who *do* evil; that is, those whose hearts and lives are aligned with the purposes of the enemy rather than being aligned with the purposes of God.

The harvesters also remove everything that causes sin. Think about it. If the harvesters are already removing all of the sinners, then why is it important to point out that also everything that causes sin will be removed? Because

---
81 Revelation 13:8
82 Romans 3:23

prior to the harvest, the people of the Kingdom may also fall into sin on occasion.

This distinction is important. The people of the Kingdom are not people who *do* evil. They are not sinners.[83] They may occasionally sin, because the things that cause sin are not removed until the harvest. But they do not normally sin, because they are by nature people of the Kingdom.

You may have a problem with the idea that the children of the Kingdom are not sinners. It may seem blasphemous to make such a claim. But it comes down to how we define sin. Perhaps you tend to think of sins as the actions we do which break the rules that God has laid out in his Word. But that is a servant perspective.

> *But He was pierced through for our transgressions, He was crushed for our iniquities; the chastening for our well-being* fell *upon Him, And by His scourging we are healed. All of us like sheep have gone astray, each of us has turned to his own way; but the Lord has caused the iniquity of us all to fall on Him. (Isaiah 53:5-6)*

These verses are an excerpt from the prophecy of the suffering servant – Jesus, who took the sin of the world upon himself on the Cross. And what was that sin? "All have gone astray, each turned to his own way." In other words, Sin is choosing to take command of your life, to protect and defend yourself, to act independently. All of the sinful actions that we may do are merely symptoms of this fundamental state of Sin. Note that this definition of Sin looks a lot like what I elsewhere have called the

---

83   They *were* sinners, prior to the death of the old man and rising to new life in baptism. But that sinner is dead. See Romans 6.

orphan spirit. And the opposite of being an orphan is truly living as a child of the King.

Until such time as the things that cause sin are removed, then the children of the King will face challenges that may lead them to occasionally fall. But each step taken as a royal child (rather than as an orphan) is a step towards strength.

Strength is built through resistance. A weightlifter will be stronger than a couch potato. And the person who has never faced a difficult decision is less well equipped to choose rightly than the one who has been trained in righteousness. In fact, where there is no resistance strength withers very quickly, as I experienced after several weeks on crutches due to a broken ankle.

And Father, in his wisdom, has chosen to allow his sons and daughters to grow strong in the presence of the enemy, the devil. The devil was thrown down to Earth[84] and imprisoned there.[85] And though the devil appears to still have some freedom to deceive people, Father is actually using him to contribute to the strengthening of the people of the Kingdom.

The fact that the devil is allowed to confront us with things that can hurt us or even lead us into sin is perhaps an unpleasant truth. How can a Good Father allow that? It is important for us to remember that *good* is not the same as *nice*. A daughter may feel that her mom is not nice when her desire to eat cake and ice cream for dinner is not met; but a good mother is more concerned about the health of her daughter than about her immediate wishes.

---

84 Revelation 12:9
85 Jude 6

As we shall see in the next chapter, the enemy is defeated through the weakness and foolishness of God. And so, when the enemy demanded to sift the disciples of Jesus[86] he was granted permission. The enemy thinks that he can damage us by sowing weeds into our field – and he might just do so if we let him uproot us – but with our eyes fixed firmly on our good and unshakable Father we become rather stronger in the midst of these weeds.

The fascinating thing is that the Son of Man apparently seems to think that there is a greater risk of uprooting the people of the Kingdom if he allows the things that cause sin to be removed before the end of the age, than if his people are allowed to grow to maturity in the presence of those things. How encouraging that he has such confidence in our future!

> To him who is able to keep you from stumbling and to present you before his glorious presence without fault and with great joy (Jude 24)

Food for thought

Do you look upon yourself as a sinner? Is that how Jesus and his Father see you? In what ways do the things that cause sin contribute to your growth and maturity?

Punishment

As we saw earlier, the attack of the enemy (sowing weeds among the good seed) ended up not being a big deal to the farmer, since he was secure in his position. But

---

86 Luke 22:31

perhaps you are left with this strange feeling that something is wrong with the picture. This enemy did a terrible thing, even broke the law, and yet got away with it.

Perhaps something inside of you would like to say, "Unfair!" Or you might think of the farmer as weak, or soft on sin. What about holiness? What about law and order? Shouldn't something be done, at least to set a precedent so that we don't have everyone attacking their neighbor and thinking it is OK?

Such thoughts are fear-based and have their root in the orphan spirit. They are entirely foreign to the thinking of an unshakable person.

The parable of the weeds starts with the statement that the Kingdom of Heaven is like a man who sowed good seed. Or to put it another way, the Kingdom is like an unshakable person. The Kingdom of Heaven is not about punishment.

It is true that the apostle Paul wrote about civil punishment. Let's take a look at that more closely:

> *For the one in authority is God's servant for your good. But if you do wrong, be afraid, for rulers do not bear the sword for no reason. They are God's servants, agents of wrath to bring punishment on the wrongdoer. (Romans 13:4)*

First, Paul says that civil authorities are servants of God for purposes of good. Then he makes a contrast. I believe that the first part of the verse speaks of the Father's good intent, while the second part of the verse is a concession to the state of civil society in a fallen world. Why do I make such a claim? Because of the concept of fear.

Paul is describing civil government, and how we should relate to civil society as believers. But he is not writing about Kingdom culture or the nature of God the King. John makes this clear in his letter:

> *There is no fear in love. But perfect love drives out fear, because fear has to do with punishment. The one who fears is not made perfect in love. (1 John 4:18)*

God is love. Thereby, his nature is neither a source of fear, nor is it primarily inclined toward punishment.[87] His nature of perfect love is constantly working to drive out fear. Consequently, punishment is not a priority.

The contrast here is between two fundamentally different ways of thinking. On the one hand you have the fear-based behavior of the orphan, and on the other hand you have the unshakable confidence of the King.

The orphan thinks and acts primarily out of their insecurity. They need to gain control of the situation, which means establishing rules, boundaries, hierarchy, etc. And, if any of these things are violated then there need to be consequences. It ends up all being about sowing and reaping. Rules become legalism, fear of losing control leads to a false sense of security by punishing the rule-breakers. People are no longer inherently valued, but instead their value is tied to their obedience to the rules. As rule-breakers lose their value, their loss becomes inconsequential, while protecting the rules

---

[87] There will be a punishment at the end of time. There *is* a lake of fire prepared for the devil and his angels, who are the primary targets of punishment. And there will also be people who choose to fall under that punishment. But that is not fundamental to the nature of the King.

gains importance. A "shoot first and ask questions later" mentality becomes acceptable. In the end, it would seem better to kill a (possibly innocent) suspect than risk an offender escaping. But who is the original killer, if not the enemy himself?

Our King is not like that at all. He is unshakable. No amount of weeds scattered in his Kingdom are able to instill fear in him. He does not need to enforce his will or his authority, because he is confident of his own nature and the accomplishment of his purposes.

The sins committed against God are not able to change who he is. He has therefore no need to react to them. He does not become more (or less) holy if he responds with anger or vengeance; or for that matter with grace. He is not answerable to our orphan-based understanding of justice.[88]

> *Truly he is my rock and my salvation; he is my fortress, I will never be shaken. (Psalm 62:2)*

Food for thought

Do you really see the God of the universe as unshakable? Or might your view of him be distorted by your own fears and insecurities? What steps can you take to see him more clearly? What is your reaction when you see someone being punished (or escaping punishment) for their wrongdoings?

The caretaker

Jesus told yet another parable that touches on the King's nature of justice:

---

88 See Hosea 11:9

> *A man had a fig tree growing in his vineyard, and he went to look for fruit on it but did not find any. So he said to the man who took care of the vineyard, "For three years now I've been coming to look for fruit on this fig tree and haven't found any. Cut it down! Why should it use up the soil?"*
>
> *"Sir," the man replied, "leave it alone for one more year, and I'll dig around it and fertilize it. If it bears fruit next year, fine! If not, then cut it down." (Luke 13:6-9)*

The first thing we need to look at with this parable is who the characters in this story represent. For many years, I read this parable and assumed that the owner of the tree represented God, the man caring for the vineyard represented Jesus, and the tree represented a person (such as you or me). However, after looking more closely, I do not believe such an assignment of roles to be true to the nature of the King.

In this parable, the owner and the caretaker of the vineyard have entirely different perspectives on the value of the tree. They are not in agreement. But Jesus said that he and his Father are always in agreement and that he always did only what he saw his Father doing. So it doesn't make sense for Jesus to tell a story where Father and Son would be in disagreement.

Jesus, in John 15:1, says that his Father is the gardener or vinedresser. And that is a role which matches very well with "the man who took care of the vineyard." And I do believe that the tree represents a person such as you or me. But who, then, does the owner represent?

One possibility is that the owner represents the accuser (the devil). After all, the owner does accuse the tree of being fruitless and wasting the soil in which it was planted. But then there is the problem of the caretaker being in a position of working with the owner. The idea of Father God working with the devil doesn't make me feel comfortable.

I think a better fit is that the owner represents the Law. Although the Law is a good thing, when combined with sin it does lead to death.[89] In this respect, it is not a problem to see Father God working with the Law and yet being in disagreement with the consequences of the Law when combined with sin.

And so, in this parable, we see the requirement of the Law demanding punishment for a lack of fruit. And we see Father God stepping in to provide extra care so that fruitfulness may have a chance to grow. This is consistent with what Jesus told us about his Father:

> *I am the true vine, and My Father is the vinedresser. Every branch in Me that does not bear fruit, He takes away; and every branch that bears fruit, He prunes it so that it may bear more fruit. You are already clean because of the word which I have spoken to you. Abide in Me, and I in you. As the branch cannot bear fruit of itself unless it abides in the vine, so neither can you unless you abide in Me. I am the vine, you are the branches; he who abides in Me and I in him, he bears much fruit, for apart from Me you can do nothing. (John 15:1-5 NASB)*

What is clear from these verses is that the key lies in abiding. To abide is to stay in contact, to remain in place, to not depart, to continue, to live. In fact, these verses

---

[89] See Romans 7:9-12

might lead us to conclude that the fertilizer in the parable represents Jesus. For the expectation of the parable is that the abundance of fertilizer will produce fruitfulness.

I would like to point out that I find the translation of John 15:2 to be a little bit misleading. Many English translations say "Every branch in Me that does not bear fruit, He takes away (or cuts off or removes)." But the Greek word translated here as "takes away," αἴρω, is a verb which primarily means "to raise up, elevate, lift up" and secondarily to carry (away) what has been lifted up. It can also imply the removal of sin.

So, an alternative reading may just as well be: "Every branch in me that does not bear fruit, He lifts it up and removes its sin." Such a reading is consistent with the message of the parable. When the requirements of the Law demand punishment for lack of fruit, Father God comes in and in essence says, "let me lift up this tree from its unfruitful condition, take away its sin, clothe it in the righteousness of Christ and provide everything necessary for it to become fruitful."

This is the nature of the King. When met with a situation that appears to deserve justice by condemnation, the Caretaker looks at the potential rather than at the results, and pours his life into that potential.

When Jesus told this parable, it was in response to an attitude based on a misconception of the nature of God.[90] It began with some folks who came and told Jesus about people who had been killed by Pilate in a horribly demeaning manner. And there was also news of several people who had died in a tragic accident.

---

90 Luke 13:1-5

In both of these cases, Jesus points out that these deaths did *not* take place because those who died were worse sinners than others. Rather, from a perspective of the requirements of the Law, everyone will perish. He then goes on, through the parable, to demonstrate that the heart of his Father is not to wipe out sinners, but rather to provide everything necessary for people to avoid perishing.

I believe that this parable and its context speaks very clearly against the idea that it is the nature of our King to bring about catastrophes in order to punish evil. Neither does he use catastrophe as a sign of his displeasure. The message of the parable is clear: The King does not desire for anyone to perish. Rather, he spends of himself extravagantly to see lack of fruit become fruitfulness.

Food for thought

What does the attitude of the caretaker of the vineyard say about the nature of the King? How does it make you feel to know that the King's eye is on your potential rather than your performance? Are you able to see other people in light of their potential?

Do you view the events in your life as a consequence of God's punishment? If so, what can you do to change the way you think?

The Kingdom

To Lose Is to Win

> *Very truly I tell you, unless a kernel of wheat falls to the ground and dies, it remains only a single seed. But if it dies, it produces many seeds. (John 12:24)*

Strangely enough, this was Jesus' reply when the disciples told him that some Greek men wanted to meet him. It was kind of an odd response to such a request, and I have often wondered what Jesus was thinking. If nothing else, it shows that Jesus' way of thinking was very different from the mainstream.

Still, this simple statement touches on a fundamental principle of how the Kingdom of Heaven works. True victory comes through apparent loss.

The kernel of wheat Jesus referred to here was himself. Once again he was making a statement about the reason he, the Son of God and the Son of Man, was walking about Jerusalem in a body of flesh: That he came on purpose to die.

The death of Jesus on the Cross was perhaps the most amazing event in the history of this world. This man Jesus, who was a popular but disruptive teacher, got on the nerves of the political and religious leadership in his country. So they killed him. What a waste, we might say.

But there was more going on. The demonic realm knew who Jesus was. Time and again, when he confronted demons that were plaguing people, those demons acknowledged him to be the Son of God.[91] And they knew Jesus was messing things up for them, so they wanted to get rid of him.

The chief priests and Pharisees also wanted to get rid of him. They were indignant because he didn't follow their rules. And they were envious of the sense of authority and legitimacy that he portrayed amongst the people. They became so enraged that they saw no alternative but to kill Jesus.[92]

The devil is fundamentally a murderer, and he influences or coerces those who are not of the Kingdom of Heaven to carry out his wishes.[93] So when the religious leaders made it their goal to have Jesus put to death they were, perhaps unknowingly, acting out the agenda of the demonic realm.

The devil is hate driven. His hatred for God and all that God loves and has created is the driving force behind everything he does. And now, here was Jesus, the beloved Son of God, walking around on Earth in a weak and limited human body, bound to the physical realm. What an opportunity for this devious scoundrel. All he had to do was convince some humans to kill Jesus and God Almighty would be put to death. An enormous victory for the devil. A sweet revenge for the humiliation that he suffered when he was cast down from Heaven.

Meanwhile, Jesus walked into his arrest fully aware of who he was dealing with and what was coming. He made no effort to escape or to plead for his rights. He had come on purpose to die. But he wasn't going to be killed, he

---

91 For example, see Mark 1:24, 3:11 and 5:7
92 John 11:47-53
93 John 8:44

was going to lay his own life down. He knew what he was doing.

The cross is a particularly nasty way to die. It is one of the most painful and tortuous forms of execution ever devised. It fits right into the agenda of the devil. And even before he was hung on the Cross, Jesus was beaten, most likely beyond recognition. Clearly, the devil was demonstrating all of his strength and power in the crushing of his enemy. For about three hours before Jesus died, the land was covered in darkness.[94] It could well be that this darkness was the manifestation of the swarms of demons that gathered in Jerusalem to gloat and celebrate.

And the Almighty God, in human form, demonstrated apparent weakness. He did nothing. He didn't resist. He submitted himself to the will of viciously destructive men and to a hateful demonic realm. And after they had done the worst they could do, he laid down his life and gave up his spirit.

Then it happened. There was an earthquake. The curtain of the temple was ripped apart. And bunches of people woke up from the dead.[95] Resurrection and life burst forth at the death of Jesus.

And the devil suddenly realized that he had made a huge mistake. What he had supposed was to be his greatest victory was suddenly revealed to be his total defeat.

---

94 Matthew 27:45
95 Matthew 27:51-52

The principle of the Cross

For the foolishness of God is wiser than human wisdom, and the weakness of God is stronger than human strength. (1 Corinthians 1:25)

The greatest victory ever won throughout all history was won through the weakness demonstrated on the Cross. All of the strength and power of the devil and all his angels, as well as that of the people he was able to deceive into carrying out his agenda, was bent on defeating God on the Cross. Instead, God at his weakest defeated and totally disarmed the strength of the enemy.

This was no accident, but rather a pivotal example of the way of power in the Kingdom of Heaven. True spiritual victory is won through weakness and loss. Greatness in the Kingdom of Heaven is measured in a totally different manner than in this world.[96]

The devil was most likely once an archangel, perhaps the highest ranking angel in the heavenlies. He is described as having been perfect in beauty[97] and having held a special position and responsibility in the presence of God. But, despite his exalted position, he reached out for more:

> *How you have fallen from heaven, morning star, son of the dawn! You have been cast down to the earth, you who once laid low the nations! You said in your heart, "I will ascend to the heavens; I will raise my throne above the stars of God; I will sit enthroned on the mount of assembly, on the utmost heights of Mount Zaphon. I will ascend*

---

96 See Mark 10:42-45, Luke 9:48
97 Ezekiel 28:12-17

above the tops of the clouds; I will make myself like the Most High." But you are brought down to the realm of the dead, to the depths of the pit. (Isaiah 14:12-15)

The root issue here is pride, wrapped in ambition. The motivation behind the actions that led to the devil's fall was a desire to achieve, grasping for that which was not offered but appeared to be within reach. To reach his goal, the devil made use of his beauty, his persuasiveness and his power in order to get what he wanted. He was out to win.

What we see here are two very different approaches to dealing with a situation:

- The "fallen" approach is to go for the win. To use the strength and power at your disposal to defeat your opponent. To succeed.

- The Kingdom approach is the opposite. To meet the challenge in weakness, fully submitted to the King, regardless of the outcome.

The "fallen" approach is also the worldly approach. Ever since the fall of man in the garden of Eden, the ways of this world have been dominated by the character of the devil, who usurped dominion through the fall. Therefore, it is common in the cultures of this world to value strength, ambition and winning. For the most part, those who rule and who influence society have gained their positions by following the "fallen" approach. In other words, their achievements are gained through use of the same methods that led to the fall of the devil.

Jesus once said, "What people value highly is detestable in God's sight."[98] And he followed up with a strange statement: that people are forcing their way into the Kingdom. This was spoken in the context of exposing the condition of the hearts the Pharisees, so I don't think that Jesus considered taking the Kingdom by force to be a good thing.[99] Taking something by force, by power, by cleverness, or the like, is operating with the mindset of the devil. It may well accomplish something in the here and now, but the eternal results will be negligible.

In Ephesians 6, Paul writes that our battle is against spiritual forces. And then he instructs us to put on the full armor of God. Have you noticed that the armor he describes is primarily defensive in nature? And after putting it all on, Paul says to stand. He says neither attack nor charge. He says: Stand.

To stand is *not* to passively let the powers of darkness walk over us. It is a very active business. We are to stand firm in the truth, exposing lies and accusations to be powerless on account of the victory of the Cross.[100] We are to take the wind out of the sails of attitudes and deceptions that would stand in the way of the knowledge of the Kingdom.[101] The simple act of resisting the devil will cause him to flee.[102]

---

98 Luke 16:15. See also: Romans 8:7, James 4:4 and 1 John 2:15-16
99 I am fully aware that there are also other valid interpretations of Luke 16:16. For example, we are called to actively pursue the Kingdom and its righteousness rather than to passively expect the Kingdom to materialize around us. More on that in a later chapter.
100 Colossians 2:15
101 2 Corinthians 10:5
102 James 4:7

As we stand against spiritual darkness, the primary weapon at hand is to speak truth in grace. Grace is not a weapon of attack, but it is the powerful and effective weapon available to us for disarming powers of darkness.

It is the devil who attacks, and he loses if only we stand firm. Because, in the spiritual realm the victory is always won through weakness and never through strength. Why would our King demean himself to operating according to the "fallen" approach of the devil?

Food for thought

What motivates you to fruitfulness? Is your approach to achieving your goals rooted in strength or in weakness, in wisdom or in foolishness? What does it mean to you to stand firm?

The power of submission

The devil's "go for the win" approach stands in stark contrast to the manner in which the victory of the Cross was won. There was no beauty, worldly wisdom or power at play on the Cross. When Jesus said, "Not as I will, but as you will," he was expressing his complete trust in the purpose and wisdom of his Father. He gladly submitted to the will and leadership of the Father. From the perspective of bringing his Father pleasure, everything else lost its value.[103]

One day, Jesus met a Roman soldier who had a sick servant. When Jesus offered to come and heal the servant, the soldier replied that it wouldn't be necessary.

---

103 See Philippians 3:7-8

Jesus need only to say the word and that would be enough.

The soldier spoke out of his understanding of the power of submission. He knew from his own experience that power and authority flow to the person who is truly submitted to the purposes of their commander. In Jesus' eyes, this demonstrated amazing faith.

There are numerous examples of the power of submission throughout the Bible, such as Moses defeating the Amelekites by raising his hands, the defeat of Jericho by marching silently, David defeating Goliath with a handful of stones, Jehosaphat defeating the Ammonites and Moabites with an army of worshipers, and so on. In each of these cases, the victory was won through the "foolish" behavior of a leader submitted to trusting God.

On two occasions,[104] God threatened to wipe out the children of Israel and start over again with Moses as the patriarch. Both times, Moses' response was, "No way. That's a bad idea, God, and you shouldn't do it. If you are gonna wipe them out, then you might as well sweep me away with them."

Most of us, given that situation, would probably have thought that arguing with God was the bad idea; and might perhaps also have been flattered by the prospect of being known throughout history as the patriarch of a great people.

But Moses didn't bite on that bait. He wasn't looking for power or for a name for himself. He was out to get a hold of God. And based on this response, God knew that he

---

104 Exodus 32:9-10 and Numbers 14:12

could trust Moses with an awesome position of leadership. As it turned out, Moses walked in enormous power and authority (though he never used it to his own gain) and he ended up with one of the most respected names and legacies in history. These were things God could grant to him because he wasn't out to get them.

Food for thought

Are you submitted to some form of leadership? If not, what is the source of authority in your life? Can you be trusted with power and authority on a greater level?

Mercy triumphs over judgment

The first time God wanted to wipe out Israel and start over with Moses, the context was judgment of the people of Israel for the sin of the golden calf. But Moses argued for mercy (just, I believe, as God was hoping he would do).

We all have a sense of justice, imperfect though it may be. Especially when someone causes us harm or loss and gets away with it, our reaction will usually lie somewhere between "that's unfair" and "they're gonna pay."

Justice and righteousness are fundamental characteristics of the nature of God. He is upright and just and does no wrong.[105] At the core, God is love. Therefore, his justice and righteousness are wrapped in goodness.

---

105 Deuteronomy 32:4

Being created in the image of God, these characteristics lie also at the core of every human's being – distorted though they may be, so many years after the fall of man.

Justice and righteousness also have a place in the being of the devil, but in him they are completely distorted. The devil, also known as the accuser of the brethren,[106] demands justice and righteousness for sinners because he knows that the wages of sin is death. And the devil, driven by his hatred of God, has set his heart on seeing everything destroyed that has any value to God. There is no good here.

The contrast between the righteousness of God and the fallen righteousness which the accuser demands pivots around the issue of punishment. An accuser demands righteousness because he gains some perverted sense of pleasure from the punishment of the guilty. God, on the other hand, views justice and righteousness (for humans) primarily through the lens of redemption and grace.

Although redemptive grace was fully released through the victory of the Cross, it has always been a part of the nature of God. He has always been the God who has no pleasure in the death of the wicked[107] and who desires that all would be saved.[108] Grace was not something that God thought up as a plan B. Rather, it is an expression of his nature of perfect love.[109]

> *Speak and act as those who are going to be judged by the law that gives freedom, because judgment without mercy will be shown to anyone who has*

---

106 Revelation 12:10
107 Ezekiel 18:23
108 1 Timothy 2:46, 2 Peter 3:9
109 1 John 4:18

> *not been merciful. Mercy triumphs over judgment.*
> *(James 2:12-13)*

From a perspective of strength, mercy seems like weakness. From a perspective of fairness, mercy seems like letting the offender win. From a perspective of control, mercy seems like being victimized. And yet, from the perspective of the Kingdom, mercy triumphs over judgment. To lose is to win.

It seems logical to us that justice and righteousness require punishment for violations of the law. But James tells us that from a Kingdom perspective we should walk the way of the law that gives freedom. What does that mean? And how does it work?

The first step toward walking in freedom is to bury our own rights. True freedom is not about exercising our rights, but about laying them down! Especially forgiveness (which is giving up our right to expect recompense when we have been wronged) plants seed that will grow into huge blessing.

Paul wrote that freedom is not about doing whatever we want to do, rather it is about serving one another in love.[110] The law of freedom may be summed up as: "Love your neighbor as yourself."

Paul also wrote about overcoming evil with good.[111] It may seem like foolishness to repay evil with good. But, as a friend of mine once said, if you fight fire with fire then you are bound to get burned. I don't recall having ever encountered a situation where repaying evil for evil brought any kind of resolution to a conflict. But extending grace to someone who doesn't deserve it (and

---
110 Galatians 5:13-15
111 Romans 12:17-21

if they did deserve it then it wouldn't be grace) goes a long ways toward defusing even the most volatile conflicts.

Actions motivated by love, grace or mercy are beyond the devil's comprehension. He operates through control, ambition, punishment, force, and so forth. He, a fallen angel, is unable to understand grace.[112] There is no grace or redemption for fallen angels – it is outside of their realm of experience. Had the devil been able to grasp the power of grace and redemption, he would have done everything within his power to prevent the death of Jesus.

Every time we speak and act along the lines of mercy rather than judgment, we are in a sense re-enacting the victory of the Cross. The enemy doesn't see it coming, because acts of grace are totally foreign to his way of thinking. When we walk in the way of grace and mercy, it makes us, in a sense, invisible to the enemy. The foolishness of the Cross becomes the law of freedom.

Food for thought

In your daily life, do you view righteousness through the lens of grace? Even when you are driving in heavy traffic? In what ways might you need to consider giving up your rights?

The value of the insignificant

In an insignificant town[113] in an irrelevant region[114] of the Middle East, the angel Gabriel was sent to visit a young

---

112 See 1 Peter 1:10-12
113 John 1:46
114 John 7:41, John 7:52, Isaiah 9:1

girl and tell her that a seed would be planted. This seed died, in a sense, when the form of God became a human baby.[115] As circumstances would have it, the baby was born in another insignificant town.[116]

A few weeks after the birth, this baby was taken to the temple to be presented to the Lord and to offer the sacrifice required by the Law. The sacrifice offered, a couple of birds (rather than a lamb and a bird), is evidence that this baby was born into a family of limited resources.[117] Most likely, their obvious lack of wealth and position meant that they went through this ritual largely unnoticed by the priests and other leaders in the temple. To his parents' astonishment, an elderly man and an elderly widow did make something of a fuss about them, but even this seems to have been disregarded by those of importance.

This seemingly insignificant birth did, however, capture the attention of some foreign magicians. They understood from the stars that a king had been born to the Jews and so they traveled to Jerusalem to see this king. But, there was no newborn king to be found among the mighty and powerful of the great city. It seems that, often, the way of God is to plant his most valuable seeds in places of insignificance.

This should not be too surprising. For the most part, those things which are considered valuable in this world have little value in the Kingdom of God.[118] And vice versa.

---

115 Philippians 2:6-7
116 Micah 5:2
117 Luke 2:24, Leviticus 12:8
118 Luke 16:15

The prophet Elijah, after defeating the prophets of baal in a dramatic showdown on Mount Carmel, fled through the wilderness in fear of Queen Jezebel. When he came to the mountain of God, the Lord asked him why he was there. Elijah began to explain about all of the significant things he had been doing for the Lord. He supposed that he was the only representative of God left in Israel, and he was a bit miffed because God didn't seem to be protecting him from Jezebel.[119]

But the Lord does not seem to have been impressed, either by Elijah's great deeds, nor by his whining self pity. Rather, he gently rebuked Elijah and gave him a bigger perspective. Elijah's mistake here was thinking that deeds of significance are a measure of value to God. In essence, Elijah was claiming that God owed him some measure of protection and safety on account of all the great things which he had done for the Lord. And this perspective blinded Elijah in such a way that he thought he was the only person who had any value to God. But the Lord had set aside for himself 7000 people whom he valued greatly, even though their faithfulness had been invisible to the prophet and the nation.

In fact, as far as we know, these 7000 people were doing more or less nothing. True, they had not bowed their knees to baal. Beyond that, we have no record of them doing anything for God, except *being* faithful. And just that appears to have been of great value to the Lord.

In the Sermon on the Mount,[120] Jesus talked about how it is the things done in secret, the things which go unnoticed, the things which appear to be insignificant

---

[119] 1 Kings 19:13-18
[120] Matthew 6

that, in the economy of Heaven, will receive their reward. And it stands to follow that the things which gain the approval of men risk losing their value from a heavenly perspective.

This is a core principle in the Kingdom of God, and a huge challenge to us in the Western Church. If our ambition is to be significant or to do significant things, then we do so at the risk of losing our value in the Kingdom of God.

Numbers lie. There is an illusion that numbers can be used to measure the significance of our work for the Kingdom of God, but that is not how this Kingdom works. We might be led to think that a congregation with thousands of members is more valuable to God than a house church with a handful of believers, but the Lord does not look at the things people look at.[121] It is not the number of people who are led to the Lord, nor the number of miracles we might see, nor the size of our church budget that touches the heart of our Lord. Rather it is the little things, the things that we turn over to him that they might die so that he can resurrect them in his time and in his way.

In the same manner, our achievements in this world need to be laid down. Paul, who had a long list of achievements to look back upon, considered those things as loss.[122] Paul rarely made use of his own titles of honor, except when identifying with others in a peer group. If we wear titles to gain attention or with an eye toward attaching more importance to who we are or to what we

---

121 1 Samuel 16:7
122 Philippians 3:4-8

are saying, then we are acting in the ways of this world rather than the ways of the Kingdom of God.

All people have a need for legitimacy. Legitimacy is the state of being acceptable, of being viewed valuable and whole within the norms of society. Those who do not gain their legitimacy from their position as a son or daughter of God will try to gain it through acts of "significance" regardless of how misguided such acts may be.

Servant leadership

In fact, Jesus said that making use of one's status or position to gain advantage or favor would be at cross purposes with Jesus' nature. Rather, the path to greatness in his Kingdom is through serving.[123] This is what Paul means by offering a living sacrifice[124] pleasing to God: Giving up your right to yourself and trusting God to make your life fruitful. The life of service is a life of freedom,[125] not because you are forced into service but because you freely choose an abandonment that leads through the death of self to a resurrection of fruitful joy in the service of the King.

In one sense, it is the life of a doormat. For we are slaves to Christ, for him to use as he would. Having turned our lives over to him, we have no rights and no claim on being treated fairly. Like the kernel of wheat falls to the ground and dies.

---

123 Matthew 20:25-28
124 Romans 12:1-2
125 Galatians 5:13

But in another sense, we are royalty: Beloved sons and daughters of the great King, heirs of God and co-heirs with Christ,[126] ambassadors of a mighty Kingdom. We must not lose sight of who we are in Christ, because it is the innate knowledge of our royal position that makes it possible for us to choose to lay aside our rights and lead through serving. Therein lies the fruitful offering with the pleasing fragrance. With a clear view of our royal position, we can choose to say, "I can afford to let that person step on me," or "I have the resources to bring life to that person in need."

To lose is to win.

Food for thought

Do you do excellent things that will go unnoticed? Is your legitimacy defined by titles, numbers or achievements? Do you measure other people by such criteria? Are you easily offended?

---

126 Romans 8:17

Identity

There is an interesting dynamic that seems to have followed Jesus. Although his teaching and his popularity had the religious leaders of his day all bent out of shape, it seems they still wanted to be seen with him. There were numerous times that Jesus was invited to the home of one religious leader or another. And more often than not, Jesus would mess with the etiquette of the dinner party and make people uncomfortable. Here is an example from a sabbath meal celebration in the home of one of the chief Pharisees:

> *When he noticed how the guests picked the places of honor at the table, he told them this parable: "When someone invites you to a wedding feast, do not take the place of honor, for a person more distinguished than you may have been invited. If so, the host who invited both of you will come and say to you, 'Give this person your seat.' Then, humiliated, you will have to take the least important place. But when you are invited, take the lowest place, so that when your host comes, he will say to you, 'Friend, move up to a better place.' Then you will be honored in the presence of all the other guests. For all those who exalt themselves will be humbled, and those who humble themselves will be exalted." (Luke 14:7-11)*

Humility

What we see here is a gathering of people in an environment where honor and respect are highly valued in the culture. That in itself is not a bad thing. But a culture where people who are something less than honorable expect or demand to be treated with honor and respect will develop unhealthy patterns of interaction.

It is clear from how Jesus sometimes addressed the Pharisees that they had developed a culture of appearing honorable without building that appearance on the foundation of an honorable heart. In Jesus' words, they were like whitewashed tombs. In such a culture, the tokens of honor become disproportionately important in order to compensate for the lack of honorable foundation.

And so we find the guests at the dinner rushing to claim the places of honor in order to appear honorable. The need to have an honorable identity led them to grab for as much honor as they thought they could get away with.

There was, it appears, an element of risk in this game: If you perchance reached too high on the ladder then you might get bumped down to the bottom by someone with enough clout to get away with publicly humiliating you. But, since everybody was playing this game, it was only natural to join in.

In the midst of this, Jesus says in essence: Hey you guys, you need to change the way you think. Because in the Kingdom of God, honor is acquired by giving it away.

In the natural world, the need to acquire honor is fed by our lack of satisfaction with who we are. If you feel that you are small and insignificant then you will naturally try to compensate by making yourself look bigger than you are. This is especially evident with dogs: Have you noticed that when you walk by a house with a small dog in the yard, it will run along the fence and yap, yap, yap at you as long as you are in the vicinity? But most often, if the yard has a large dog it will just lay there on the porch and hardly give you more than a look (unless you try to climb over the fence). Small[127] people tend to do the same thing – they just bark in a different manner, which we might call self-promotion.

In good Christian circles, we might have the tendency to swing the pendulum too far the other way. In order to snuff out any hints of self -promotion there can in its place arise a culture of demeaning and devaluing people in the name of humility. When humility is defined as a reaction to unhealthy self-promotion then it becomes an equal but opposite tool for destruction of the soul.

I define humility as a healthy mix of two things:

- *Releasing control:* Admitting to yourself that you are inadequate to manage the full scope of your life, and turning that control over to your Lord.[128] Not relying on your own strength, but honoring with your trust and dependency the One who has the strength, love and wisdom to present you faultless before his throne.[129]

- *Embracing truth:* Knowing who you are in Christ. Being so secure in your position as a beloved,

---

127 By "small" here, I am *not* referring to physical stature, but rather to smallness of identity.
128 1 Peter 5:6-7
129 Jude 24

accepted and sanctified son or daughter of the King of the universe that you have nothing to prove. Having such confidence in your value that you can freely waive your rights. Allowing others to "steal" the honor that is your due because you know that they can't actually touch your inherent value.

From this position of humility, it is a piece of cake to attend a dinner party with Jesus. You know that his favor is upon you, so you can sit anywhere in the room. You know that he is in control, so you can be sure that you will get enough to eat. You know that he is good, so it is your pleasure to watch him be good to others.

Motivation

Jesus followed up with a challenge to his host:

> *Then Jesus said to his host, "When you give a luncheon or dinner, do not invite your friends, your brothers or sisters, your relatives, or your rich neighbors; if you do, they may invite you back and so you will be repaid. But when you give a banquet, invite the poor, the crippled, the lame, the blind, and you will be blessed. Although they cannot repay you, you will be repaid at the resurrection of the righteous." (Luke 14:12-14)*

This illustrates another side of the same issue. Remember that Jesus had a tendency to embarrass and irritate the Pharisees in public. So it is not too long of a stretch to guess that this Pharisee's motivation for inviting Jesus to dinner had a lot more to do with being seen with Jesus than actually wanting to spend time with him.

Jesus goes right to the root. The nature of his Father is to send blessing on both those who deserve it and those who do not.[130] So the identity of a citizen of his Kingdom is demonstrated in a generosity and freedom which springs out from the abundance of the King.

In this Kingdom, our actions should not be motivated by what we can gain from doing them. Rather, as our hearts are filled with Kingdom identity, we act out of the position of the Kingdom – its wealth, its bounty, its grace.

This position of wealth is really fundamental. When we truly understand our identity as sons or daughters in an abundantly wealthy Kingdom, then it is easy to be motivated by generosity. If we have the mistaken idea that there aren't enough resources to go around then our natural response to any given situation of need will be negative. But, as we gain revelation of our identity as wealthy subjects of a wealthy Kingdom it becomes our nature to give without any expectation of return because we can think, "I can afford to do this."

Passion

On another occasion, Jesus was one of several guests invited to dinner at the home of a Pharisee named Simon. During the meal a woman of questionable reputation showed up and made things a bit uncomfortable.

Sometimes I wonder how she got into the house. After all, if she was known in that town for her sinful life, why did she have access to this Pharisee's home? And why did the host or his servants let her carry on at the dinner party? I don't know. But for some reason she was not

---

130 Matthew 5:45

chased out. Instead she wept and kissed and anointed the feet of Jesus in a dramatic demonstration of passionate gratitude.

When Jesus perceived his host's inner thoughts, which went along the lines of: "If Jesus really were the hot shot he claims to be, he would put a stop to this sinful woman's outrageous behavior," then Jesus dropped a parable on his host.

> *"Two people owed money to a certain moneylender. One owed him five hundred denarii, and the other fifty. Neither of them had the money to pay him back, so he forgave the debts of both. Now which of them will love him more?" (Luke 7:41-42)*

When it was put that way, the answer was fairly obvious: The one who was forgiven more will have a greater measure of appreciation for the value of that forgiveness.

But then Jesus brings it home:

> *"Do you see this woman? I came into your house. You did not give me any water for my feet, but she wet my feet with her tears and wiped them with her hair. You did not give me a kiss, but this woman, from the time I entered, has not stopped kissing my feet. You did not put oil on my head, but she has poured perfume on my feet. Therefore, I tell you, her many sins have been forgiven—as her great love has shown. But whoever has been forgiven little loves little." (Luke 7:44-47)*

Jesus compares this sinful woman's outrageous behavior to the common expressions of hospitality (in that culture) that one would expect of their host if the host truly wanted them to feel welcome: allowing a guest to wash their feet before entering the home, welcoming them with a token of affection, and treating them with an appropriate measure of honor.

Simon had not honored his guest with any of these tokens. But this woman who had forced her way into the premises had touched on all three with an extravagance and passion that made the host and the other guests feel uncomfortable and perhaps a bit inadequate.

But the woman didn't care. Undoubtedly, she knew quite well what her reputation was in the eyes of the respectable people of that town. And she knew how little she deserved to gain the notice of this radical rabbi (Jesus) who was visiting Simon the local Pharisee. But something touched her heart deeply, and stirred in her an understanding of her identity as a lover of God: a worshiper.

I find it interesting that in this setting Jesus more or less erases the importance of sequence. In the case of the two debtors, the one loves more as a consequence of the forgiveness. But in the case of the woman, he says that her many sins are forgiven because of her passion.

If our perspective of the Kingdom of God is primarily judicial in nature, then our understanding of grace will be limited to the grace that our actions deserve (which is really a contradiction in terms). But if our perspective of the Kingdom is primarily framed in love then we will more easily see that love knows no bounds. Sometimes it is the grace of God that releases thankfulness, while other times it is the revelation of who we really are created to be that releases grace. Jesus had more faith in this woman than anyone else present, including the woman herself, because he knew what she was created to be. Therefore he spoke to her words of acceptance, "your sins are forgiven," and words of revelation, "Your faith has saved you; go in peace."

Whether it is forgiveness that releases passion or passion that releases forgiveness, they will both speak into our identity to the degree that we allow. Jesus' statement that "whoever has been forgiven little loves little," can be revealing. If we live under the illusion that we didn't need very much forgiveness, then it will become evident through a lack of passion. Without passion we run the risk of joy in our life being replaced by legalism and servanthood. In other words, passion is a key ingredient in maintaining an identity of sonship.

Food for thought

Are there habits in your life that are designed to make you appear more honorable? Can you afford being disrespected? *Are you wealthy? Are you quick to think generously? What are you passionate about? Do you rejoice in extravagant acts of worship?*

Grace and Works

One day, a wealthy young man came to Jesus and asked what he needed to do to gain eternal life. The reply Jesus offered was perhaps more costly than he had expected, and he departed in sadness. This led Jesus to observe that the wealthy will find it difficult to enter the Kingdom of Heaven; a statement that knocked the disciples off balance.

Why? Because the Kingdom of Heaven is basically upside-down compared to our natural understanding. Or it might be more accurate to say that our world is what's upside-down. In any case, we have a natural tendency to think that material blessing is an indication of heavenly approval. But Jesus' point is that, in the Kingdom of Heaven, what appears to be first is last and what appears to be last is first. And to further illustrate this, he told a parable:

> *For the Kingdom of Heaven is like a landowner who went out early in the morning to hire workers for his vineyard. He agreed to pay them a denarius for the day and sent them into his vineyard. About nine in the morning he went out and saw others standing in the marketplace doing nothing. He told them, "You also go and work in my vineyard, and I will pay you whatever is right." So they went. He went out again about noon and about three in the afternoon and did the same thing.*
>
> *About five in the afternoon he went out and found still others standing around. He asked them, "Why*

have you been standing here all day long doing nothing?"

"Because no one has hired us," they answered.

He said to them, "You also go and work in my vineyard."

When evening came, the owner of the vineyard said to his foreman, "Call the workers and pay them their wages, beginning with the last ones hired and going on to the first." The workers who were hired about five in the afternoon came and each received a denarius.

So when those came who were hired first, they expected to receive more. But each one of them also received a denarius. When they received it, they began to grumble against the landowner. "These who were hired last worked only one hour," they said, "and you have made them equal to us who have borne the burden of the work and the heat of the day."

But he answered one of them, "I am not being unfair to you, friend. Didn't you agree to work for a denarius? Take your pay and go. I want to give the one who was hired last the same as I gave you. Don't I have the right to do what I want with my own money? Or are you envious because I am generous?" So the last will be first, and the first will be last. (Matthew 20:1-16)

It seems as though everyone has an understanding of what they think is fair, but that understanding is usually based on their feeling of what is unfair. It doesn't take very long after a child learns to speak before they start claiming that "it's unfair" when things don't go their way.

Nearly every time we feel that things are unfair, it is because we have compared our circumstances with those of someone else. From something as simple as "she got a bigger piece of cake than I did" to systematic and repeated acts of injustice, the act of comparison can greatly influence our feelings. And seldom is that influence positive.

In this story, the workers expected to be paid according to their works. Those who were hired first figured that, since those who had only labored the tail end of the day were rewarded with a denarius, they would receive a greater reward for their greater works. When that didn't happen, they were quick to cry, "unfair!"

The landowner, on the other hand, was true to his promise, that each worker would be paid what he considered right. By his standard, anyone who was working in his vineyard at the end of the day received the same payment.

This landowner, who illustrates an aspect of the nature of Father God, demonstrates a value system that might just make you want to cry, "unfair!" And that should be no surprise, because grace *is* unfair. Completely, and totally unfair.

In fact, we tend to have a strange relationship to grace. It is easy enough to receive grace yourself, while at the same time perhaps feeling a touch of irritation when others come off getting better than they deserve. Or perhaps you find yourself trying to earn what you have received by grace, and tend to act (though you may not have thought of it that way) as though God owes you something for your efforts. Either way, grace ends up leaving us feeling a little bit uncomfortable, because it doesn't fit well into a common understanding of what is right. The problem here is that our common understanding of righteousness is actually a rather ugly thing. "What people value highly is detestable in God's sight."[131]

Grace is the currency of the Kingdom of Heaven. When the landowner paid all of the workers "whatever is right," they were not paid according to their works, but according to their position at the end of the day. This landowner is not so much concerned with how much his workers do for him as he is interested in where they are in relationship to him.

In a framework of grace, everyone is equal: equally valuable and at the same time equally incapable of earning their position in grace. With this background, making comparisons between people based on outward things, such as what they do or what they have done or what they have, is an insult to the nature of the One who gives grace. Or, as the landowner said, "Are you envious because I am generous?" Whether our thought is that someone received more than I did, or that someone else received something I wanted, or that I ought to have received more for my effort, such lines of thinking are actually expressions of greed and distrust toward our Father in Heaven.

This business of comparing is deeply rooted in the nature of fallen man. Its source is in the nature of the fallen angel, Lucifer, who despite being perfect in beauty made it his ambition to take hold of more than he had been

---

131 Luke 16:15

given. Although each of us as Christians have become a new creation in Christ, we may still need to unlearn these kinds of habits and thought patterns.

The Bible touches on the subject of comparing from a number of different perspectives. We are warned about covetousness and greed,[132] which is actually a form of idolatry that makes us an enemy of God. The disciples of Jesus were frequently found "discussing" which of them was the greatest, leading Jesus to point out that greatness in the Kingdom of Heaven is not measured by outward deeds, but by having a heart of a service.[133]

But it goes even farther than this. One of the most insidious forms of comparison is the idea that different automatically means better or worse. This is the subject of 1 Corinthians 12, where Paul wrote about there being different spiritual gifts with different purposes. But, as he emphasizes, it is not that one gift is more valuable than the other. Rather, he describes the different gifts as being like the different parts of a body. The goal is a body that moves and functions well together, in health and harmony. In a harmonious body, you will never find a hand that wants to be an eye.

Which brings us back to the landowner. Perhaps his aim was more far reaching than simply gathering a pack of laborers for a day. It could well be that he was out to build a team who would be committed to the goals of his vineyard over the long term, and who would work together harmoniously to achieve those goals.

---

[132] For example, see Exodus 20:17, Luke 12:15, Ephesians 5:5-6, James 4:2-4
[133] See Matthew 18:1-4, 23:11-12, Mark 9:33-37, Luke 9:46-48, 22:24-26

The complaint of the workers who were hired first ("you have made them equal to us") is very much like the complaint of the prodigal son's older brother to his father when he refused to go in to the feast ("All these years I've... but when this son of yours..."). Clearly, the older brother feels that his father's behavior is unfair. In essence, he is saying, "Look at all the things that I have done to be acceptable in your eyes! How can you possibly show grace to this rogue who deserves punishment, without rewarding me for my works?"

To start with, this complaint demonstrates a preference for judgment, which is an unacceptable position to take in the Kingdom of Heaven. As James put it, "judgment without mercy will be shown to anyone who has not been merciful. Mercy triumphs over judgment."[134] Rather, we are called to minister restoration and forgiveness to those who have broken the rules. Paul put it this way:

> *Brothers and sisters, if someone is caught in a sin, you who live by the Spirit should restore that person gently. But watch yourselves, or you also may be tempted. Carry each other's burdens, and in this way you will fulfill the law of Christ. If anyone thinks they are something when they are not, they deceive themselves. Each one should test their own actions. Then they can take pride in themselves alone, without comparing themselves to someone else, for each one should carry their own load. (Galatians 6:1-5)*

The complaint of the first-hired workers (and of the older son) is also an example of what I call entitlement. Entitlement is the idea that someone owes me

---

134 James 2:13

something. It leads me to think that I deserve something because of what I have done or who I am. When I don't get what I believe I am entitled to, a seed of bitterness is planted. And bitterness stands in opposition to grace.[135] In fact, Jesus said that many "on that day" who, in their surprise that they were found to have not done the will of the Father, would stand before him and point to their miraculous deeds as evidence of their entitlement. But his response will be, "I never knew you."[136]

When the prodigal son's father replies to the older son, it is as though he is speaking an entirely different language. He doesn't even address the issue of his sons' deeds (whether good or bad). Rather, his response is entirely relational: "You are always with me, and everything I have is yours. But we had to celebrate and be glad, because this brother of yours was dead and is alive again; he was lost and is found."[137]

This father was clearly a father to his sons. He loved them unconditionally, both the son who was rash and disobedient, selfish and wasteful; and the son who mistakenly tried to earn his father's acceptance through good behavior. But I suspect that as long as they measured their relationship to him in terms of their own performance, both sons brought far less joy to their father than he would have liked.

Sonship is not only a matter of knowing and acting on your position as a son rather than a servant. Sonship is also about *being* a son or daughter to your father. Being a son involves getting to know the heart of the father and incorporating what lies on his heart into your own life.

---

135 Hebrews 12:15
136 Matthew 7:21-23
137 Luke 15:31-32

At the same time, being a son involves letting the father get in touch with your own heart. The will of Father God is not only for you to know and experience him, but also that he gets to know and experience you.

There is a tricky balance here, and it is easy to miss the point if you are influenced by a deeds and rewards mentality. It is a little bit like a multi-faceted diamond – the beauty comes from seeing the jewel with its many facets rather than focusing entirely on one side.

- Your position as a son or daughter of our heavenly Father is sure. He chose you before the foundation of the world.[138]

- There is nothing you can do to make God love you more. Neither is there anything you can do to make him love you less.

- He, who knows the end from the beginning,[139] has chosen you and loves you with a full knowledge of who you are, what you have already done and what you will yet do.

- Several times, Jesus spoke of loving him and keeping his commands.[140] He did not say that you must keep his commands to earn his love. Rather, keeping his commands is a fruit of loving him and a help to remain in his love.

- He delights in you because you are you.

---

138 Ephesians 1:4-5
139 Isaiah 46:10, Jeremiah 1:5
140 For example, see John 14:15,21, 15:10, see also 1 John 5:2-3, 2 John 1:6

- Your affection to him brings him pleasure. His passionate desire is for his Spirit to feel at home in you.[141]

Grace says that you can't change how much God loves you and delights in you. But your works can influence the degree to which you bring God pleasure. Not if you are doing works to please God, but when your desire to know him and bring him pleasure results in good works that spring out from that desire.

One of the things that has brought me pleasure as a parent is to see the things which are dear to my heart reflected in the character of my children.[142] That's what happens when a child spends time with their parent with an open heart. Or as one of my favorite songs of worship puts it:

> *I want to sit at your feet*
> *Drink from the cup in your hand*
> *Lay back against you and breathe*
> *And feel your heartbeat.*[143]

Food for thought

Does it make you uncomfortable when people go unpunished? Do you feel bothered if your efforts go unnoticed? What is the opposite of envy? What does it mean to be known by God?

---

141 James 4:5
142 It's a little bit different when I see hints of the things I'm less satisfied with in myself, but Father doesn't have that problem.
143 From "The More I Seek You" by Zach Neese, © 1999 Gateway Create Publishing

A Culture of Freedom

One day, Peter came to Jesus with a question: "How many times do I have to forgive my brother who sins against me?" After having traveled with Jesus for a while, Peter had clearly understood that forgiveness was an important part of Kingdom life, and he had probably begun to understand the ocean of forgiveness for his own sin that Jesus was making available. But Peter had grown up in a rules-based, "you reap what you sow" kind of religious system. So his question was really more along the lines of: How big *is* this forgiveness thing? When is enough enough? Where is the boundary between grace and judgment?

In response, Jesus told the following story:

> *Therefore, the Kingdom of Heaven is like a king who wanted to settle accounts with his servants. As he began the settlement, a man who owed him ten thousand bags of gold was brought to him. Since he was not able to pay, the master ordered that he and his wife and his children and all that he had be sold to repay the debt.*
>
> *At this the servant fell on his knees before him. "Be patient with me," he begged, "and I will pay back everything." The servant's master took pity on him, canceled the debt and let him go.*
>
> *But when that servant went out, he found one of his fellow servants who owed him a hundred silver coins. He grabbed him and began to choke him. "Pay back what you owe me!" he demanded.*

> *His fellow servant fell to his knees and begged him, "Be patient with me, and I will pay it back." But he refused. Instead, he went off and had the man thrown into prison until he could pay the debt.*
>
> *When the other servants saw what had happened, they were outraged and went and told their master everything that had happened. Then the master called the servant in. "You wicked servant," he said, "I canceled all that debt of yours because you begged me to. Shouldn't you have had mercy on your fellow servant just as I had on you?" In anger his master handed him over to the jailers to be tortured, until he should pay back all he owed.*
>
> *This is how my heavenly Father will treat each of you unless you forgive your brother or sister from your heart. (Matthew 18:23-35)*

Jesus starts by saying, "The Kingdom of Heaven is like a king.." At first glance, you might think that this king represents God, but it seems to me that the symbolism in this story is far more complex. I think that, to begin with, the king represents you or me – someone who wants to settle accounts, someone who wants their losses recompensed. After the servant (who could also represent you or me) fails to walk in forgiveness, we might think that the king represents God the judge, and to a certain extent this may be true. But for the most part this is not so much a story about the nature of Father God as it is a story about how forgiveness and freedom work together. In essence, I believe that this story is demonstrating two different approaches to dealing with offense or debt – a Kingdom of Life approach and a servant of darkness approach.

Still, the implication of this story is clear: In order to function in this Kingdom, you need to learn to think and act in accordance with the culture of the Kingdom. So let's walk through the story.

The king has a servant who owes an impossible debt; something on the order of the national budget. There is obviously no way that it can ever be repaid. So the king orders that this servant should suffer the loss of everything in order for the king to recover some symbolic measure of his own losses.

In his desperation, the servant asks to be given time to make good his debt. Both he and the king are well aware that this is an empty promise. But this pitiful request from a servant, who in reality has absolutely nothing to offer, touches the heart of the king. And the king responds by canceling the entire debt and releasing the servant from the suffering he was due.

The servant, however, failed to learn from his master's example. When he shortly afterward ran across a friend who owed him quite a bit of money (a few months wages), he required judgment even though his debtor promised to pay if only he was given time. When word about this got back to the king, he was enraged and punished the servant severely.

So what was it that enraged the king? It was the servant's failure to walk in the culture of his kingdom.

There is no evidence of anger during the servant's first meeting with the king. Rather, there was an atmosphere of hope in a hopeless situation. But the wrath of the king is revealed in the second meeting. And it appears that this wrath is directed, not at the debt, but at the debtor's insistence on continuing to walk in a lifestyle that keeps account of debts when he had been invited into a culture of freedom.

This pattern was also demonstrated in Jesus' life. The sinful actions of people did not anger him. Rather, his wrath was aroused on the occasions when he was faced with people or situations (or unclean spirits) which held people captive to legalism, disease or demonic oppression.

So, when Peter asked how many times a man should forgive, he was asking the wrong question. The whole business of keeping a record of wrongs is foreign to the nature of this Kingdom. In such a culture, you can't ask how many times to forgive, because there is no record of the wrongs[144] previously forgiven. You can always forgive once, and you end up never actually counting to two.

The culture of the Kingdom brings restoration. When the king forgave the debt, he forgave it completely, and released his servant to live as if the debt had never existed.

This Kingdom culture is about freedom – freedom from shame, freedom from condemnation, freedom to live unburdened, and more. But attempting to live with the benefits of a culture of freedom while still desiring to burden those around us with condemnation and shame, is an enormous violation of that culture.

In a rules-based culture, lives are validated by their ability to follow the rules. If a rule is broken at some

---

144 1 Corinthians 13:5

point, then the consequences must be paid. If a king in such a culture were to fail to require due punishment for the broken rules, then the people of the kingdom would feel violated. The failure to sustain the authority of the rules through the judicious application of appropriate punishment will eventually lead to a collapse of that culture.

A freedom-based culture, however, is built on the relationship between a good king and his followers. It is their love for their king that drives the people to live their lives in a way that brings their king pleasure. They are not required to follow rules, but their desire to please the king leads them to learn the ways of the king and walk thereafter. The king does not demand obedience, but why would his followers choose to disappoint him? So, freedom reigns because love leads to obedience without coercion or manipulation.[145] In this context, demanding punishment for a broken rule violates the culture by destroying the foundation of love on which the culture rests.

> *The wrath of God is being revealed from Heaven against all the godlessness and wickedness of people, who suppress the truth by their wickedness, since what may be known about God is plain to them, because God has made it plain to them. (Romans 1:18-19)*

When the servant had his friend imprisoned, the king responded to his servant in wrath. This happened only after the king had first made the true nature of the kingdom plain to his servant by forgiving the enormous debt. Wickedness in this context is experiencing the

---

145 See John 14:15

truth of God's goodness, and yet walking in a way which suppresses that truth. You can't expect to reap the benefits of a culture of freedom without learning to walk out your life in that same culture.

But don't let that frighten you. It takes a lifetime, or more, to learn to walk in all the ways of godliness. It is not as if God is out to get you if you trip up along the way toward learning more about his ways. What matters is a desire to follow his heart.

Food for thought

Is the culture of your home more rule-based than freedom-based? Do you keep record of the wrongs you have experienced? Do you view punishment as an adequate solution to wrong-doing? Are your actions or attitudes toward those who may have offended you at risk of suppressing the truth of God's goodness?

Forgiveness

Forgiveness is a fundamental aspect of walking into a culture of freedom. So it is important to understand something about what it is and how it works.

First of all, in order to forgive, there has to have been a real offense. You don't need to forgive me if I give you a hundred dollars. But you would probably need to forgive me if I ran up from behind and pushed you face first into a mud puddle. That may seem like a no-brainer, but here's the point: It is the issues where we have truly suffered loss or been hurt or injured that require forgiveness. We may think about the so-called unforgivable sin,[146] but in practice it is only where there has been no loss that there is no place for forgiveness.

So, we have a situation where somebody deserves judgment. A rule has been broken or an offense has been made, or a debt exists, or whatever. Our sense of righteousness calls for punishment. In our pain we may desire revenge, which we imagine will somehow repay some of our loss, even though the offense may seem so incredibly large that there is no hope of repayment.

And this situation raises its ugly head in the midst of the King's culture of freedom. What is to be done? Well, what have we learned from our King? How does he meet these kinds of situations? Obviously, we are called to forgive.

Now forgiveness is not pretending like it never happened. Neither is forgiveness acting as if it was OK after all. It was *not* OK; there *was* an offense and losses were suffered. Those things may take time to heal.

Forgiveness is saying, "I cancel the debt." It is setting the offender free from the requirement of repayment, restitution or punishment for the pain that was inflicted or the loss that was incurred. Or, more correctly, it is relinquishing the right to require recompense, and turning it over to the only person with sufficient wisdom to handle the case in a manner worthy of the culture of the Kingdom: the King himself.

Whether you declare these things before Papa God in your own heart, or also speak them to the offender may be a difficult decision. The purpose of forgiveness is freedom, so that should be a guiding principle in choosing the specifics of how to communicate

---

146 Whatever that is, it is *not* a sin that has been committed against you or me. See Matthew 12:31-32 and Mark 3:28-29.

forgiveness. If the offender is unlikely to understand or acknowledge the offense, then often speaking forgiveness to the offender will more likely lead to misunderstanding, anger or confusion than lead to freedom.

Forgiveness is not an emotional thing, even though we may go through a lot of emotions in the process. Forgiveness is a heart issue, where the love of God which is shed abroad in our hearts leads us to proclaim freedom in the face of the accuser. It may take an act of the will for you to choose to develop a forgiving heart, but when the decision is taken there, the practice of forgiving from the heart will grow in fruitful soil. It may be that you need to remind yourself of your act of forgiving multiple times in order to establish the decision in your mind and emotions, but the deeper the roots of forgiveness grow in your heart, the easier this will become.

One of the most common emotions we need to deal with when we have been hurt or offended is anger. Unresolved anger gives the devil a foothold.[147] A foothold is a place that gives an opportunity to stay attached. In other words, if we don't deal with our anger, then we allow demonic power to establish a foundation in our life where it has the right to stand. Forgiveness is like a sledgehammer that smashes the foothold and causes the devil to lose his grip. Forgiveness may seem unfair or impractical, but it releases freedom by pulling up the source of anger at its root.

The enemy of our souls, the devil, is also called the accuser of our brothers and sisters.[148] Often in a situation

---

147 Ephesians 4:27
148 Revelation 12:10

calling for forgiveness, the voice of the accuser is there demanding "righteousness" in the form of punishment. You may not actually hear a voice in your head (most people don't). But have you considered that, when facing a decision to forgive, you tend to meet a barrage of thoughts about what the person has done, how offended or hurt you are, and so on? That is the accuser at work.

The jailers and torturers in the final scene of this parable represent the accuser. Because the barrage of accusations flooding our mind will continue, if we do not forgive. This barrage has several goals, including: To keep the wound open and festering, to get you to agree with the accusations, and occasionally also to remind you how inadequate you are for having not forgiven. Not much freedom in that. And as long as you are in agreement with these accusations, they will have a controlling influence in your life.

So perhaps even more than setting the offender free, forgiveness brings freedom to the person offended. And it opens the door to healing, by cleansing and closing the wound that the accusations have infected.

Food for thought

In what ways has your understanding of forgiveness been changed by the definition presented here? Is there some bitter root of anger or offense that has been keeping you from walking in freedom? Are there accusations that are influencing your thought patterns today?

The third party

There is one specific kind of offense situation which deserves a closer look, because this one is especially disruptive to a culture of freedom. If John hurts Mary, and Peter takes offense on Mary's behalf, this becomes what I call the third-party forgiveness problem. Since John has hurt Mary, the Kingdom culture course of action is for Mary to forgive John. But the same obvious course of action does not exist for resolving the offense that Peter carries. John didn't hurt Peter (as far as John knows), so he won't see the need to ask Peter for forgiveness.

Frequently in these kinds of situations, John and Mary resolve the situation between them, forgiveness is given and freedom is released. But the handful of people around Mary who have taken upon themselves an offense which they do not own, sit with that festering wound and become prisoners of the accuser. And, as time goes by, shame, pride and bitterness build up and make forgiveness even more difficult.

The parable at hand gives some insight in how to deal with this kind of situation. When the servant turned his friend over to judgment, the other servants of the king were offended. But rather than holding on to their offense (thus giving food to the accuser), they immediately took the situation to the king and turned it over to him. They told the king what they had experienced and how they felt about it. And then they released the situation, trusting their king to handle it in wisdom.

In the final analysis, the culture of freedom is about trust. Do I feel that I need to deal with the offenses, hurts or losses that I encounter in my own strength and seeming wisdom? Or do I trust the King to protect me? To restore me when I have been hurt? To manage grace and righteousness in a manner worthy of his Kingdom? The person who trusts is able to walk free from fear and worry.

Food for thought

Are you carrying any third-party offenses?

Passing on the blessing

Shouldn't you have had mercy on your fellow servant just as I had on you? (Matthew 18:33)

Another aspect of a culture of freedom is passing on to others the blessing which you have received. It stands to follow that the people of this Kingdom ought to be the most merciful and forgiving people in the world. Unfortunately, that is not always the picture that the world has of the church.

At the most basic level, the moral law of reaping what you sow[149] causes blessing to follow those who pass on the blessings which they have received. This is a mechanism that works both inside and outside of the Kingdom of God.

For example, I believe that much of the blessing that followed the United States through the latter part of the 19th century and well into the 20th century was released by the fact that the borders were pretty much open, allowing people to come from all over the world and take

---
149 Galatians 6:7

part in that blessing. And I suspect that the transition during the past half century to more closed borders is perhaps restricting the flow of blessing over that country. For also nations will reap what they sow.

The transfer of blessing is the currency of the culture of freedom. Every action and transaction is paid for by passing on blessing. Freely you have received; freely give.[150] When we encounter blessing, we repay with blessing. When we encounter resistance we repay with blessing.[151] When we are cursed we respond with blessing, because you can break off a curse,[152] but a blessing cannot be broken. Where grace abounds, there is no such thing as an undeserved blessing. The more we walk into this culture of freedom, the more naturally we become sources of blessing to others. And the more people around us experience blessing, the more freedom they will encounter – thereby drawing them into the culture of freedom as well.

A concrete example: On occasion I may loan money to somebody. I have a standard 3-point set of terms for loans:
1. It is a loan. The borrower is responsible for repaying the loan. But it is up to the borrower to set the repayment schedule according to their own means.
2. I charge no interest. The amount borrowed is the amount to be repaid.
3. I encourage the borrower to do likewise for someone else when the need and opportunity arises.

---

150 Matthew 10:8
151 Matthew 5:38-42
152 Proverbs 26:2

These terms are designed to bless the borrower, to give the borrower freedom while at the same time encouraging and empowering them to walk responsibly, and to lead the borrower into the practice of passing on the blessing.

I have a selective memory, so there have been times when I have forgotten about loans which I have made. A number of years ago, I got an e-mail from a high school friend asking for my postal address, because she wanted to send me something. I was a bit surprised, since I hadn't heard from her in years. What came in the mail was a check repaying some money she had borrowed at least 10 years earlier; a loan that I had totally forgotten about. Needless to say, I was really blessed by her faithfulness.

But passing on the blessing is not just about money. It is primarily about becoming like our King. The more we look upon the King, the more like him we become. And the more people will experience the blessings of God flowing through us toward them.

Food for thought

List five or ten ways that you have been blessed in the past year. What can you do to pass on blessing that you have received?

Restoration

What do you think? If a man owns a hundred sheep, and one of them wanders away, will he not leave the ninety-nine on the hills and go to look for the one that wandered off? And if he finds it, truly

> *I tell you, he is happier about that one sheep than about the ninety-nine that did not wander off. In the same way your Father in Heaven is not willing that any of these little ones should perish.* (Matthew 18:12-14)

At first glance, this parable is a picture of the compassion of God and the value system of Heaven. The paradox is that the person who returns from the brink of destruction releases more joy than those who never ventured out from under the safety of the Father's wings. While, at the same time the act of walking out of that safety brings the Father more pain and distress than we can comprehend.

This is true. But there is more to be found here. Many Bible publishers have added headlines or titles which are not a part of the actual text. There are no headlines, titles or paragraphs in the original Greek. If your Bible has headlines, they have been added to aid you in locating specific texts. Unfortunately, many translations use headlines to divide this chapter into several segments; thereby breaking up a context which actually ought to be looked at as a whole.

To start with, Jesus was defining greatness in the Kingdom of Heaven: That it is childlike wonder and humility which opens the gateway into the Kingdom and paves the way to favor and honor there (verses 1-5). Most likely, one of his goals was to, once again, try to put an end to the constant vying for position that was going on between his disciples.

He then followed up by stating in very graphic terms how highly this childlike nature is valued in the Kingdom. It is so highly valued that we should go to great lengths to make sure that nothing gets in the way of the childlike person entering or abiding in the Kingdom (verses 6-9).

And, to make it a little more specific, he said in verse 10 that we should be sure not to have any negative feelings toward "these little ones," whom he also defined as "those who believe in me."

So the background that led Jesus to tell this parable is tied to the simple, childlike faith of the believer; and to their safety, which is protected by their Father whose face shines upon them. And in particular that they should be protected from anything that could separate them from the Kingdom, especially disputes with one another. It is on this basis that Jesus in verses 15-20 interprets the parable.

> *If your brother sins, go and show him his fault in private; if he listens to you, you have won your brother. But if he does not listen to you, take one or two more with you, so that by the mouth of two or three witnesses every fact may be confirmed. If he refuses to listen to them, tell it to the church; and if he refuses to listen even to the church, let him be to you as a Gentile and a tax collector. (Matthew 18:15-17 NASB)*

Unfortunately, some have extracted verses 15-17 from the surrounding context in order to use them as "a biblical pattern for church discipline." And, not surprisingly, applying this pattern out of context rarely produces results that see the missing one restored to the ninety-nine in an atmosphere of joy.

The key is found in verse 14: The Father does not want to see any believer outside of his protection. Since the parable is about sheep, perhaps you don't quite catch how strongly the Father feels about it. But, imagine a kindergarten teacher who takes a hundred children on a field trip. If she comes home and says, "Well, I brought ninety-nine of them back with me; that's pretty good, isn't it?" you might begin to feel the panic that would strike the parents of that one child, and the wrath that would arise in them toward the teacher. "In the same way your Father in Heaven is not willing that any of these little ones should perish."

With this background, Jesus described a 3-step pattern for how to move forward when you have been offended:

1. Verse 15: Talk it out one on one. If that works, you have gained your brother.

   The goal of this talk is restoration. It is not anywhere nearly so important to establish the facts of any sin that has been committed (though it will usually be necessary to work through them at some point during the process of restoration) as it is to communicate forgiveness to the offender.

   Hopefully, this will be the only step necessary. If you walk into it with the attitude of bringing the offender into safety, then that person will be far more receptive than if they fear condemnation or conflict.

   The phrase "won your brother" can be a bit misleading. Other translations use "gained your brother."[153] The point is that you should not be out to win an argument or debate, but you should be out to win back a close relationship.

---

153 The NIV translation of "won them over" is particularly misleading.

2. Verse 16: If step one didn't work, try again with one or two trusted mediators.

   This verse also quotes the principle from the Mosaic Law that a case must not be decided on the basis of testimony from only one witness. If you lose sight of the context of restoration, it might be easy to conclude that the function of these witnesses is to bring testimony (in step 3) about the sins of the offender. But that is not the case at all.

   The function of two or three witnesses is elaborated in verses 18-20. We will come back to that shortly.

   The one or two mediators that you take with you should be people who are trusted by both parties, so that there will be an atmosphere of safety. Remember that the goal is to bring one lost and insecure sheep back into a secure position in the presence of the shepherd.

3. Verse 17: If step two didn't work, then it might be necessary to involve a wider scope of people. If all fails, we should treat them as a person in great need of grace and forgiveness.

   This is a tricky business, since we humans have a natural tendency to prefer gossip over restoration. Once again, if we forget that the Father's primary motivation is that none of these little ones should perish, then this step can cause irreparable damage.

Note that with each step it becomes increasingly important to stay focused on the heart of restoration on which this process is founded.

> *Truly I say to you, whatever you bind on earth shall have been bound in heaven; and whatever you loose on earth shall have been loosed in heaven. Again I say to you, that if two of you agree on earth about anything that they may ask, it shall be done for them by My Father who is in heaven. For where two or three have gathered together in My name, I am there in their midst. (Matthew 18:18-20 NASB)*

In these verses lie the key to restoration. And it is tied to forgiveness. When we go to the offender, whether alone or in the company of one or two mediators, it is we who hold the power to bind the sin to the offender or to release them from its penalty. Consequently, we also hold the keys to the outcome of the process (whether or not it may immediately appear to be so).

Looking back at the things that may cause one of these little ones to stumble: When two or three of us are gathered together, and Jesus is present with us, how tragic it must be for him if we choose to bind the sin to the offender rather than releasing them through an act of forgiveness.

The owner of the sheep was only concerned about the fact that the one sheep had wandered away. It made no difference what reason or circumstances had led the sheep astray. Even if the sheep had willfully defied his owner and left the flock, the owner's focus was entirely on restoring the sheep to safety.

Food for thought

How can you tell if you are binding a person's sins to them? What feelings does that generate inside of you? Is there someone you need forgive or be reconciled with? If so, what steps can you take to begin restoring that relationship?

The One Thing

> *The Kingdom of Heaven is like treasure hidden in a field. When a man found it, he hid it again, and then in his joy went and sold all he had and bought that field.*
>
> *Again, the Kingdom of Heaven is like a merchant looking for fine pearls. When he found one of great value, he went away and sold everything he had and bought it. (Matthew 13:44-46)*

Chances are you may never have been in the position where you would gladly give anything and everything just to get a hold of something that seemed out of reach. Maybe you've been close, you've thought you might be willing to give it all, but it just didn't happen that way.

I recall once driving our 9-year-old daughter and some of her friends to a birthday party. Along the way, one of the girls was talking about her cell phone[154] and some of the other stuff that she had. And then she said that she would gladly be without that stuff if only her parents got together again. And she probably meant it. But she also knew it was more a sigh of hopelessness than something she had any realistic chance of seeing happen.

That is a fairly typical example of the kind of situation where we say that we would give everything. But it's a passive expression. Rarely do we actually act upon the thought. So these kinds of situations are not really

---

[154] This was before "everyone" had a cell phone.

representative of what Jesus was talking about in these two parables.

The man in the field and the merchant stumbled upon something that they immediately recognized as having great value. And so they went into action. Not only did they think, "I would give everything to get that," but they actually invested the time, planning and effort to give everything.

The Kingdom of Heaven is something that makes everything else fade in value. It is the one thing worth gaining. In light of that one thing, the value of everything else pales in comparison.

Although salvation is freely given to everyone who would believe in the Lord Jesus Christ, the Kingdom of Heaven does have a price. Of course, Jesus paid an enormous price on the Cross to gain the victory that made forgiveness of sins available to all mankind. But in order to really gain the value of this grace, there is an additional price to be paid: you must give up everything.

> *For whoever wants to save their life will lose it, but who-ever loses their life for me will find it. (Matthew 16:25)*

These parables might be looked at from God's perspective. Imagine God browsing through all of the planets in the universe, until he came upon the Earth. There he found a treasure buried in a pearl whose surface was covered with beings created in his own image. Despite the dirty sin that covered these people, God the Father sold that which he most valued, himself, God the Son, in order to purchase this costly pearl. In fact, he not only purchased this buried treasure, but also all of the dirt that was covering it. Possessing this one thing for himself remains the focus of his attention and affection. There is a truth here, but the parables also call *us* to similar extravagance.

I assume that if you have read this far into this book, then you consider yourself to be a Christian. But why? What was your motivation for choosing to believe? What do you expect to be the reward for your faith?

- Are you after fire insurance? Is avoiding the flames of hell sufficient motivation to sell everything? Are you hoping to get to Heaven simply because it sounds like a better place to end up than in hell?
- Are you after a bath? The blood of Jesus washes us completely clean from all sin and shame. But is that all there is?
- Are you after a cosmic vending machine? Did you figure that becoming a Christian would solve all of your problems and meet all of your needs? That, if only you ask, you will get whatever you want?
- Are you after a trophy? Do you expect to be rewarded in Heaven for the good you have done on Earth or for the things you have suffered?

The truth is that none of these things alone have enough inherent value to be a pearl of great price. At least not for a whole lifetime. It takes something more to be worth selling everything.

I believe that, at the most basic level, everyone wants to be truly loved, to have significance and to experience fulfillment in their lifetime. We may not have thought these things through, or we may express them in different ways, but these are fundamental human needs that spell out the difference between simply surviving and living an abundant life.[155]

We are created in the image of God. So it stands to reason that these basic desires are a reflection, imperfect though they may be, of what lies on the heart of God. God is love so, of course, he desires to love and to be loved. There is nothing and no one more significant than God, but the value of significance is multiplied when there is someone with whom to share the experience. And though God is infinite and complete, it gives him great fulfillment when beings choose, of their own free will, to love him.

So how do we go about experiencing love, significance and fulfillment? In the economy of the Kingdom of Heaven, in order to possess that which is freely given, we must pay the price of everything. Usually, the value we place on something reflects the cost that we have paid. We tend to value that which costs us nothing exactly that much. Grace is freely given, but if you really want to gain its full value then you need to sell everything.

One day, Jesus was visiting two sisters in their home.[156] The one sister, faithful to the prevalent expectations for good hospitality, was hard at work getting things prepared so they could have a proper visit. But as she worked her irritation grew toward her sister, who simply sat in the presence of this visitor and hung on to his words. Finally, she could hold it in no longer so she went to Jesus and asked him to tell her sister to behave herself properly. What was Jesus' reply to her? There is really

---

155 John 10:10
156 Luke 10:38-42

only *one thing* that is necessary, and your sister has discovered it.

So what is this one thing? Well, spending time in the presence of God is a part of it. But the presence is not the goal itself. The goal is getting to know and experience the One who is present. Being in his presence is probably the best way to get to know his nature and to have it rub off on you.

When an object is placed in the presence of a very strong fragrance, with time that fragrance will permeate the object. Eventually that object becomes a carrier of the fragrance. While her sister was preparing lunch, Mary was soaking up fragrance. She didn't seem to be doing anything useful, but clearly Jesus felt that she was doing something valuable.

This is one aspect of what Jesus was talking about when he said[157] to set your focus on getting a hold of his Kingdom, one consequence of which would be that all the trappings of daily life would fall into place. Seeking his Kingdom is not about finding a glorious place to live some time in the future. Rather it is about getting to know the King and learning so much about him and all that surrounds him that we become immersed into his culture so that it leaks all over those around us.

One of the Old Testament paradoxes which fascinates me, is that God both forbade and welcomed his people into his presence. This God is both fearful and wonderful, full of grace and holy beyond description.

One aspect of the holiness of God is that there can be no sin in the presence of God. His wrath is kindled by

---

157 Matthew 6:33

wickedness. And yet, at the same time he is the God whose desire is that no one should perish.

The Old Testament solution to this problem was the Tabernacle. The Tabernacle was a tent with two rooms and several layers of coverings. Around the tent was a fence. All of which was there to insulate a holy God from sinful people.

With a few exceptions, nobody was allowed to even go near the fence. Of those few who were allowed inside the fence to do the necessary work there, only the priests could enter into the outer room of the tent, and that only at the prescribed times of the day. The inner room, where the presence of God (represented by the ark of the covenant and the mercy seat) did dwell, was off limits to everyone except the high priest. He could only enter once a year and only in accordance with very specific rituals. It was such a risky business, that they usually tied a rope around this priest's ankle, in case it became necessary to drag his dead body out.

But there was another tent, outside of the camp, where Moses would go to meet with the presence of God face to face. When Moses met the Presence there, everyone else kept their distance, bowed down each at the entrance of his own tent. Except for a young boy named Joshua, who apparently spent his days just being there in this tent of meeting.[158]

Years later, a young boy named Samuel found himself in the service of the high priest of his day. Although Samuel was not of priestly heritage, he wore the clothing of a

---

158 Exodus 33:7-11

priest and served in the presence of God. In fact, he even slept in the inner room beside the ark of the covenant.[159]

Fast forward another generation or so. A young man named David has become king. This David, also known as a man after God's own heart, can not bear the thought of governing his kingdom without having the presence of God and the ark of the covenant near him in the capitol city. His first attempt to bring the ark up to the city ended in catastrophe when someone reached out and touched the ark (to steady it from tipping over) and died on the spot.

They parked the ark at the home of a guy named Obed-Edom for a few months. This ended up completely turning things upside-down for Obed-Edom, who spent the rest of his life going wherever the ark went. This passion for the presence of God appears to have also rubbed off on his sons.

After David finally got the ark into the city, he set up a tent for it. There is reason to believe that this tent did not have two rooms and may not have had any walls at all. David's instruction was that musicians and singers should perform acts of joyful worship there in the tent every day and night without ceasing.

Why was it that Joshua, Samuel, Obed-Edom and David's worshipers could break the rules and stay in the presence without fear? What had they grasped that made them immune to the wrath of a holy God?

A closer look at how the rules came about gives some insight. When the people of Israel came to Sinai after escaping from Egypt, God said to Moses that he was

---

159 1 Samuel 3:3

inviting *all* of the people to be his own possession, to be a kingdom of priests.[160]

A few days later, they all went out to the foot of the mountain to meet with their God. It was an overwhelming experience. While God was giving Moses the Ten Commandments, the mountain was enveloped in smoke and thunder and lightning. And this nation of newly liberated slaves was, understandably, filled with fear.

Their fear led them to tell Moses that they didn't want closeness to God.[161] The concept of having a relationship with their Lord was quite foreign to them. They were used to being told what to do by their masters. So that was how they figured they wanted to relate to God as well. If they could just have a bunch of rules to follow, they could handle that. They would relate to their Lord (and try to please him) by following instructions. That seemed to be a lot easier than actually getting to know this terrifying God.

And then, to these ten commandments were added hundreds of rules, regulations and instructions. And the culture of rules that grew around them spawned even more rules, so that by the time Jesus walked in Jerusalem the Pharisees were enforcing nearly three times as many rules as those spelled out in the Law of Moses.

The Law is a good thing when it draws the hearer to a closer understanding of the heart of God. But those who receive the Law with a slave mentality tend to think they can gain acceptance by following instructions, which ends up increasing separation from God the Lawgiver. Or,

---

160 Exodus 19:5-6
161 Exodus 20:19

as Jesus said, "You search the Scriptures because you think that in them you have eternal life; it is these that testify about Me; and you are unwilling to come to Me so that you may have life."[162]

Still, God is a God whose nature does not change, and his desire for relationship with his people was not erased by the arrival of the Law. So, for those who discovered his nature and chose to draw near on the basis of his goodness, the door was open to enter into relationship. But, for those who would attempt to draw near within the framework of following the rules, the rules did still apply.

Jesus said that the time of the Law and Prophets ended with John the Baptist. Since that time, the doorway to press in to relationship is thrown wide open.[163]

What is the point? It appears as though God allows, perhaps even encourages, rule breaking when it leads to relationship.[164] Or, as Paul put it: "He has made us competent as ministers of a new covenant—not of the letter but of the Spirit; for the letter kills, but the Spirit gives life."[165] Moses, Joshua and Samuel all made contact with the Spirit of God and learned to relate to him in Spirit and truth. The tragedy is that so many of us, out of our fear that we may die from getting too close to God, would rather relate to him through the letter of the Law (which kills).

---

162 John 5:39-40 NASB
163 Luke 16:16
164 Don't misunderstand here. This does not mean that sin doesn't matter.
165 2 Corinthians 3:6

The key to changing tracks lies in actually taking the initiative to do so. It is not enough to find the pearl of great price; you have to actually sell everything in order to gain it. It is not enough to follow all of the rules and hope that God notices you. If you really want to become a person after the heart of God, then you have to abandon the propriety of trying to please him by your behavior and run the risk that he might just burn you to a crisp when you recklessly throw yourself into his presence.

One of the problems with a rules-based relationship is that it feeds the spirit of entitlement. By that, I mean the idea that I deserve something because of something I have done. It could be something as broad as "God has to bring me to Heaven because I held his commandments," or as specific as "I fasted yesterday so why haven't you answered my prayer?" Anything that may lead us to think that we are entitled to something, that we have a right to something, that the system ought to do something for us, is influenced by this spirit.

But the currency of the Kingdom of Heaven is grace. And, although grace is freely given and can not be earned, it must be received in order for the transaction to take place. In other words, the opposite of entitlement is taking responsibility.

There was the time Jesus walked on the water and was actually planning to pass by his disciples and leave them struggling in the boat.[166] An entitlement perspective would expect Jesus to come to the rescue of his disciples. But, as Bill Johnson has said, sometimes the Lord only comes near enough to scare you. The question is, what are you going to do about it?

---

166 Mark 6:48

Jesus is the Son of God, the perfect representation of Almighty Father himself. Even so, he learned obedience through the things which he suffered.[167] Think about it! The God of the universe is all-knowing, eternal and omnipresent. And yet there was something that he *learned* by going through a temporal process.

If we walk in a culture that avoids suffering, then we also miss out on something worth learning. A pearl is formed through irritation,[168] and a pearl of great price is not formed without cost. The Kingdom of God is not something that simply happens to us, but something we must pursue. And that pursuit has its price.

> *"Suppose one of you wants to build a tower. Won't you first sit down and estimate the cost to see if you have enough money to complete it? For if you lay the foundation and are not able to finish it, everyone who sees it will ridicule you, saying, 'This person began to build and wasn't able to finish.' Or suppose a king is about to go to war against another king. Won't he first sit down and consider whether he is able with ten thousand men to oppose the one coming against him with twenty thousand? If he is not able, he will send a delegation while the other is still a long way off and will ask for terms of peace. In the same way, those of you who do not give up everything you have cannot be my disciples. (Luke 14:28-33)*

The cost of being a disciple of Jesus is nothing less than everything. Which may leave you wondering if it is worth

---

167 Hebrews 5:8
168 A pearl is formed when some foreign object enters a shellfish, which then protects itself by surrounding the object with hard, smooth material.

it. No one can make that decision for you. You need to calculate the cost and weigh it against the benefits. If you have not found the pearl of great price, then no amount of enthusiasm or encouragement on the part of other people will be sufficient to carry you to the end of the race.

It is a little bit like getting married. One cost of getting married is forsaking all others for the sake of building an intimate relationship with that one person who has captured your heart. Is it worth it? I would say yes.

Since the creation of this world, the Father has been about the business of preparing a suitable bride for his Son. That bride, the Church, includes you. Just a look from your eyes takes his breath away.[169]

Food for thought

What is your prime motivator, that one thing, for following Jesus? Does it bring you joy? What kinds of things are able to compete with that one thing?

Do you feel that God owes you something for your service to him? Do you find yourself grumbling when things don't go the way you expected? What remains then to be sold?

---

169 Song of Solomon 4:9

The Business of Doing Church

Jesus was teaching in the temple, and the chief priests were upset. Just the day before, Jesus had come riding into town on a donkey ("presuming" to be the prophesied king[170]) and raised quite a ruckus by disrupting business in the temple, healing the blind and the lame, and letting children run about and make a racket. The chief priests had been beside themselves with rage.

And here he was again. So they challenged his authority to teach. After all, in their system of understanding, authority in the temple came from hereditary and academic credentials. And they knew that this ragged carpenter from Nazareth had none.

But Jesus threw them a curve by linking his authority to the authority behind John the baptist, whom the crowds held to be a mighty prophet in their own day. This presented the chief priests with something of a dilemma. Though they did not acknowledge the unconventional ministry of John, they were afraid to say so publicly.

And while the chief priests were standing there feeling trapped between their rage and their fear of the crowds, Jesus told them this parable:

> *"What do you think? There was a man who had two sons. He went to the first and said, 'Son, go and work today in the vineyard.'*

---

170 Zechariah 9:9

> " 'I will not,' he answered, but later he changed his mind and went.
>
> "Then the father went to the other son and said the same thing. He answered, 'I will, sir,' but he did not go.
>
> "Which of the two did what his father wanted?"
>
> "The first," they answered.
>
> Jesus said to them, "Truly I tell you, the tax collectors and the prostitutes are entering the Kingdom of God ahead of you. For John came to you to show you the way of righteousness, and you did not believe him, but the tax collectors and the prostitutes did. And even after you saw this, you did not repent and believe him." (Matthew 21:28-32)

What Jesus is saying here is that appearances do not always reflect reality. For example, appearing to be religious without actually having a heart that is aligned with the heart of the Father will not bring the Father pleasure. The religious leaders of Jesus' day (and perhaps ours as well) were like the second son – giving lip service to the father, but not actually producing fruit in accordance with the father's desire. Most likely, the majority of them started out truly intending to serve their God. So why no fruit?

Both in relationship to his own authority and in explanation of the parable, Jesus referred to John the Baptist. He said that John came to show the way of righteousness. The core of John's teaching was a calling to "bring forth fruits in keeping with your repentance"[171]

---

171 Luke 3:8 NASB

rather than relying on outward things such as hereditary or academic credentials. But the religious leaders were blind to such a message.

> *All the people, even the tax collectors, when they heard Jesus' words, acknowledged that God's way was right, because they had been baptized by John. But the Pharisees and the experts in the law rejected God's purpose for themselves, because they had not been baptized by John. (Luke 7:29-30)*

These verses show that there was a connection between the baptism of repentance[172] and a person's ability to internalize the ways of God. Those who received the baptism of John were better equipped to see beyond the religious traditions of their day into the Kingdom that Jesus represented. The baptism of repentance cleansed their hearts so that they could change the way they thought. But those who rejected the baptism of John had no such advantage. They were predisposed to cling to their traditions.

John the Baptist was the son of a priest. He had been raised under a strict regime and spent his days isolated in the desert. Even so, when he appeared publicly, he was hardly conventional, dressed in rough-hewn garments and eating the food of a wild man. Needless to say, the established leaders in the temple were not impressed. And the fact that he called them names and threw accusations at them when they came to check him out, certainly didn't make his teaching any more attractive to them. So they were in no mood to receive his call to repentance.

---

172 Acts 19:4

The problem was that the priests and Pharisees were convinced that their own righteousness was measured by their rituals and status. Though some were probably corrupt, many had little idea of the huge gap between their outward behavior and the kind of Kingdom life that the God of Israel longed for. The result was that they did not produce the fruit of repentance.

In the parable of the two sons (above), the fruit of repentance is portrayed as the produce of working in the vineyard. The work of the vineyard is to nurture and harvest fruit that brings joy and pleasure to the landowner.

> *"Listen to another parable: There was a landowner who planted a vineyard. He put a wall around it, dug a winepress in it and built a watchtower. Then he rented the vineyard to some farmers and moved to another place. When the harvest time approached, he sent his servants to the tenants to collect his fruit. The tenants seized his servants; they beat one, killed another, and stoned a third. Then he sent other servants to them, more than the first time, and the tenants treated them the same way. Last of all, he sent his son to them. 'They will respect my son,' he said. But when the tenants saw the son, they said to each other, 'This is the heir. Come, let's kill him and take his inheritance.' So they took him and threw him out of the vineyard and killed him. Therefore, when the owner of the vineyard comes, what will he do to those tenants?"*
>
> *"He will bring those wretches to a wretched end,"* they replied, *"and he will rent the vineyard to*

other tenants, who will give him his share of the crop at harvest time." (Matthew 21:33-41)

In this parable, the tenants were doing the work of the vineyard, but in the process of doing that work they lost sight of the vineyard's purpose. It was the landowner who established the vineyard. It was he who insured its security and provided for its well being. In fact, he was the one who gave the tenants a home and a purpose. We can assume that at the time they made their agreement with the landowner, the tenants fully intended to provide the landowner with the fruit he expected to receive.

But when the time came for harvest, the tenants failed to live up to their promise. Apparently, they were so consumed with their own achievements, their own sense of satisfaction at having produced some fruit, that they were unwilling to give the landowner his due for the foundation he had laid.

As time went on, their self-sufficiency began to get the better of them. Their failure to recognize the calling of the vineyard led them from arrogance to abuse to murder. Most likely they had no intention of becoming murderers when they first engaged in the business of the vineyard. But that is where their choices led them.

Why? One reason may be that they looked upon the fruit which they had produced as a token of status or accomplishment. It is easy for us to get the idea that achieving measurable results is the goal of Kingdom life. But I do not believe that to be the case. Rather, I believe that the process is far more valuable to Father God than the results are. The fruit that the landowner actually longs for is much more the process of doing things together than it is the things we may accomplish for him.[173]

And yet, rather than building their relationship with him, the tenants made it their ambition to become like the landowner[174] by cutting off the owner's legacy. But how could such wanton destruction achieve the destiny for which the vineyard was created? Like the son who said he would work the vineyard but didn't, these tenants worked the vineyard but failed to produce the fruit that the landowner expected.

> *My well-beloved had a vineyard on a fertile hill. He dug it all around, removed its stones, and planted it with the choicest vine. And He built a tower in the middle of it and also hewed out a wine vat in it; then He expected it to produce good grapes, but it produced only worthless ones. ... Thus He looked for justice, but behold, bloodshed; for righteousness, but behold, a cry of distress. (Isaiah 5:1b-2,7b NASB)*

The landowner was looking for justice and righteousness. Instead, he received bloodshed and distress, which culminated in the murder of his own son. How did this come about? I believe that a major factor was that the tenants did not pursue a close relationship with the landowner, thereby leading them to value things which the landowner did not value. When the messengers from the landowner arrived, they defended their choices and became indignant rather than returning to the purpose and destiny of their original agreement.

---

173 See John 15:4-5
174 A terrible goal. See Isaiah 14:14

> Jesus said to them, "Have you never read in the Scriptures:
>> 'The stone the builders rejected
>> has become the cornerstone;
>> the Lord has done this,
>> and it is marvelous in our eyes'?
>
> "Therefore I tell you that the Kingdom of God will be taken away from you and given to a people who will produce its fruit. Anyone who falls on this stone will be broken to pieces; anyone on whom it falls will be crushed." When the chief priests and the Pharisees heard Jesus' parables, they knew he was talking about them. They looked for a way to arrest him, but they were afraid of the crowd because the people held that he was a prophet. (Matthew 21:42-46)

Just like the tenants in the parable, when the religious leaders heard Jesus tell this story, they responded with indignation. Their hearts were so far from the heart of God, and their actions were so different from what the Lord they claimed to represent was expecting that they walked directly into the fulfillment of the parable.

Indignation

It is quite a revealing exercise to follow the instances of offense and indignation through the Gospels. On several occasions, the people – and especially the religious leaders – reacted with indignation or fury to the way Jesus and his disciples behaved. Here are some examples:

- Early in Jesus' public ministry, he visited his hometown. The people there knew him and his family. They knew that he didn't have any religious credentials. But, there he was, teaching with wisdom and performing miracles. Matthew and Mark say that this offended the people. Luke says that they were so offended that, in their fury, they tried to kill Jesus.[175]

- Jesus liked to spend time with tax collectors and sinners. He ate and partied with them, to the extent that he was ridiculed as a glutton and a drunkard. He even chose a tax collector to be one of his twelve disciples. This offended the religious leaders.[176]

- It also bothered them that Jesus healed people. Perhaps they were a bit envious, since they weren't seeing any miraculous healings in their own ministry. But, what really made their blood boil was when Jesus healed on the Sabbath.[177] On one occasion, Jesus healed a man born blind. The Pharisees were so annoyed by this man's testimony of "I was blind but now I see" that they insulted him and had him ejected from their presence.[178]

- In fact, they tended to insult anyone who was willing to listen to Jesus, rather than blindly following the Pharisees' narrow-minded understanding of the Law.[179]

- Jesus referred to himself as the bread that came down from Heaven. This offended the people,

---

175 Matthew 13:54-58, Mark 6:2-3, Luke 4:28-29
176 Luke 5:29-30, 7:34, 15:1-2, 19:5-7
177 Luke 6:9-11, 13:14
178 John 9:24-34
179 John 7:47-52

because they knew him to be the son of Joseph.[180] When he went on to use imagery of eating his flesh and drinking his blood, even his disciples were offended.[181] In both cases, Jesus said that no one can come to him unless the Father enables them.

- Not surprisingly, the Pharisees and the teachers of the Law didn't like it when Jesus pointed out their hypocrisy and their confidence in ritual performance.[182]

- When Jesus entered the temple on what we now call Palm Sunday, he was followed by a noisy and joyful crowd. They were shouting things like "Hosanna!" and "Blessed is the king who comes in the name of the Lord!" And people were being healed and children were running about. It was a bit of a circus. The religious rulers were indignant and asked Jesus to rebuke his disciples for their seemingly inappropriate behavior.[183]

- Once at a dinner party, a woman came in and poured out a whole bottle of costly perfume on Jesus' head. Some of the disciples were indignant at this recklessly wasteful act of worship.[184]

Do you see what these examples have in common? In each case, people were indignant or offended by actions that didn't fit their understanding or expectations of

---

180 John 6:41-44
181 John 6:53-65
182 Matthew 13:3-14, Luke 11:37-54
183 Matthew 21:14-15, Luke 19:37-39
184 Matthew 26:6-9, Mark 14:3-5

proper sacramental behavior. At times, their indignation so aroused their wrath that they tried to kill Jesus.

Indignation is usually a symptom of the religious spirit. The religious spirit is a devious thing, because it replaces relationship with system. It sets up requirements for behavior, which create bondage rather than freedom. And ultimately, the religious spirit is out to destroy the heir in order to take possession of the vineyard as its own.

The religious spirit

Two passages in the prophets[185] describe a beautiful and powerful being who once walked in the presence of God. But pride and arrogance led to wickedness, with the result that this being was cast down to Earth. This being, adorned with stones reminiscent of Aaron's priestly garments, had a central position in the worship of God. But his own beauty and splendor led him to make it his ambition to become like the Most High.

And so this being, once the seal of perfection, is now the devil, the enemy, the destroyer, the deceiver, the accuser. He wanted to take over the vineyard for his own purposes, but was instead thrown down and stripped of his beauty and splendor.

That beauty and splendor had reflected the God who created him. When he was thrown down, he was totally separated from God. In other words, every aspect of beauty, splendor, wisdom and goodness was removed from him. What was left was hatred, darkness and destruction.

---

185 Isaiah 14:12-15 and Ezekiel 28:12-17

In particular, he hates God. And as a consequence, he hates life, beauty, wisdom, peace and anything that would remind him of the beauty and splendor that once was his. He hates everything that the Lord loves, especially humans.

But he was not stripped of his memory. He who once walked among the fiery stones has not forgotten what it means to stand in the midst of the presence of the Lord, and how that glory elicits true worship.

This being, who still desires to be like the Most High, understands worship. One of his highest priorities is to destroy the worship of the Lord and, where possible, to redirect it toward himself. Which is why the religious spirit is so devious and destructive.

Religion is defined as: a set of beliefs concerning the cause, nature, and purpose of the universe, especially when considered as the creation of a superhuman agency or agencies, usually involving devotional and ritual observances, and often containing a moral code governing the conduct of human affairs.[186] There are especially two aspects of this definition that are the domain of the religious spirit:
- Devotional and ritual observances, and
- Governing the conduct of human affairs.

These two aspects of religious behavior lead to bondage rather than freedom, by prescribing specific behavior instead of nurturing a living relationship.

Carrying out devotional and ritual observances is a bit like the son who said he would go to work in the

---

186 religion. Dictionary.com. Dictionary.com Unabridged. Random House, Inc. http://dictionary.reference.com/browse/religion (accessed: Sept. 01, 2015).

vineyard, but did not actually do so. The goal of ritual observances is to become acceptable to God, in order to avoid his wrath or in order to gain some benefit. Ritual observances have the appearance of sacred behavior without actually bringing pleasure to the Lord.[187]

The religious spirit also encourages the enforcement of a moral code to govern the conduct of human affairs. This has two goals:
- When people have a set of rules to follow, they don't need a relationship with their leader, and
- A set of rules is designed to limit behavior rather than to encourage freedom.

A moral code usually includes many good and admirable practices. The devil is not opposed to righteous behavior, especially when it results in alienating people from God. The farmers in the vineyard did a good job of managing the vineyard and producing its fruit. But their practice of farming led them to cut off their relationship to the owner of the vineyard.

The best counterfeit is the one that is most nearly like the real thing. And the devil, with his first-hand knowledge of true worship in the presence of God Almighty, is quite adept at influencing religious practice to have all of the appearances of holiness while at the same time failing to deliver the fruit that brings pleasure to the Lord.

For example, the Bible – the Word of God – is described as being like a sword. A sword is a useful and effective tool in the hands of a skillful swordsman. But it can also be a source of wanton death and destruction when wielded

---

[187] See 1 Samuel 15:22-23, Isaiah 1:11-17, Matthew 9:13, Colossians 2:20-23

by a barbarian. The Bible is full of truth, but for truth to be fruitful, it must be wielded in the spirit for which it was intended. When the truth of the Bible is used to bring condemnation on people, the result will be death and destruction. This is the religious spirit in action: There is an appearance of placing a high value on the Word of God, but the underlying motivation is egotism cloaked in indignation, and the fruit is anything but pleasing to the Father.

In the same manner, there are a myriad of religious traditions and practices out there. Some, such as the rituals of other religions or cults, we may easily see as expressions of the religious spirit. Far more damaging are the practices that we embrace within our own congregations. Please don't misunderstand me here. I am not opposed to traditions or to worshipful behavior that encourages, welcomes and strengthens the relationship between the Living God and his beloved children. The key, again, is motivation. Religious practices that are motivated by a desire to be more righteous, a need to be acceptable, or an attempt to exclude or punish those who are outsiders are most likely driven by the religious spirit. How different things turn out when the practice of worship is focused on giving to the landowner the fruit that he desires.

Food for thought

What is the fruit of the vineyard that brings pleasure to the landowner? In what ways might you be holding that fruit back for yourself?

What kinds of actions lead you to react with offense or indignation? Do you have any religious habits that don't produce fruit that brings pleasure to the Lord? Are there rules or guidelines that you follow in such a manner that it gets in the way of your relationship with the Father?

Do you handle the written word of God skillfully as a surgeon or do you perhaps wield it as a barbarian? What are some ways that worship brings pleasure to God?

The landowner

The purpose of a vineyard is to produce fruit that results in good wine. So, what exactly is this fruit that the landowner desires? I see four specific things in the new testament:
- He longs for his Spirit to dwell in his children[188]
- He seeks worshipers who worship in spirit and truth[189]
- He wants all people to be saved and learn to know the truth[190]
- He desires to join with his bride in unity[191]

All of these four longings are about the relationship between a Father and his children or a Bridegroom and his bride. In other words, it is about people rather than practices. It is about relationships rather than rituals. And it is more about *being* than about call and vision. This is the fruit of the landowner's vineyard. For the love between this Bridegroom and his bride is better than wine.[192]

---

188 James 4:5
189 John 4:23
190 1 Timothy 2:4
191 John 17:21-24
192 Song of Solomon 1:2

> *My people have been lost sheep; their shepherds have led them astray and caused them to roam on the mountains. They wandered over mountain and hill and forgot their own resting place. (Jeremiah 50:6)*

The challenge facing us in church life is how to keep "the business of doing church" from causing us to withhold the fruit of the vineyard from the landowner. Or, as Jeremiah put it, the work of a good shepherd is to bring the sheep to a place of rest.

Jesus said that he only did what he saw the Father doing.[193] In other words, he demonstrated the behavior of the Father. Or, as the writer of Hebrews put it, Jesus is the exact representation of God.[194] So, the best way to observe how to go about producing the fruit of the vineyard is by looking at how Jesus did it.

Being with people

First of all, Jesus spent a lot of his time just being there with people. He liked people and a lot of his time was spent in the midst of people doing the things people do in their daily lives. He ate and drank with them. You might say he was something of a party animal. On at least one occasion, when the party ran out of wine, he made more. In fact, he was even accused of being a glutton and a drunkard. And for the most part, he did this with people who were not necessarily respectable. He was also derided for being a friend of tax collectors and sinners.

---

193 John 5:19
194 Hebrews 1:3

Sometimes when I stand in a crowded bus or walk through the streets of the city, I ponder the fact that the Lord knows and loves every one of these individuals that are crowding around me. He sees their problems, their pain, their longings, their dreams, and their destiny. And he cares.

I have to admit that I don't have the capacity for that. I usually manage to ignore the majority and be polite to those with whom I interact. I might even have a thought about how it would be good for them to get to know Jesus. But I am not wired to actually relate in depth to very many people. It is much easier for me to tend to get caught up in the business of doing church than it is for me to really face all of the people I meet and actually care about their dreams or problems. But I have discovered that it is easier to care about people I spend time with than it is to care about those I simply meet or pass by in a crowd situation.

Have you noticed how the people around Jesus felt loved? John, for example, called himself the disciple that Jesus loved. Martha and Mary were beloved friends. Zacchaeus was so touched that after just a meal with Jesus he was ready to turn his life and finances upside-down. When Jesus hung out with folks, he made them feel seen, wanted, accepted and whole.

I may be able to do that with a few people, but not very many and not all of the time. And that seems to be the case for most of us. Creating an environment where the people around you feel loved is certainly one of the behaviors that Jesus modeled. It is an aspect of the nature of God, and should be demonstrated as clearly in his body (we, his followers; the Church) today as it was when he walked the streets of Jerusalem.

When Jesus said that he and the Father are one, and that he did only what he saw his Father doing, it stands to reason that one of the things he saw his Father doing was being a Father. In other words, when Jesus related to people, it wasn't just a matter of solving their need and moving on to the next person. Jesus wants to build an intimate relationship with each individual person. He wants to be a part of bringing them out of their pain and into a mature, mutual, and delightful fellowship with himself.

A pastor friend once made this observation about another pastor in our city: His church will never grow to be larger than about 40 people, because he wants to *know* all of the members in his congregation. My friend, who was thinking mostly in terms of church growth, didn't necessarily see that as a positive characteristic. But I wonder. Is successful church leadership really measured in how many people can be gathered? Or might it rather be measured in the depth and quality of relationships that are developed between the people in a fellowship and their God and between one another?

For most Christians, their pastor(s) and other church leaders are the most influential role models they have for learning how to live life in the Kingdom of Heaven. Whether a leader is conscious of this or not, it is the portion of their lives that is seen by the congregation that will most influence their congregation's understanding of what kind of fruit the landowner is expecting to harvest.

When the congregants only know the segment of their pastor's life that is demonstrated from the platform, they might easily be led to believe that platform ministry is the normal lifestyle in the Kingdom of Heaven. But that does not match at all with how Jesus lived his life. The gospels only record about 50 of the 1000 or so days of Jesus' public ministry. If Jesus spent a fair share of those 50 days just being together with people, how much more so on the days whose events didn't get recorded in the gospels.

What people really need to see is that the radical and life-changing principles of the Kingdom of Heaven actually work in their daily lives. And the best way to see that happen is for our pastors and teachers to live a lifestyle that is open and transparent. For example, we don't need so much to be told, "Husbands, love your wives as Christ loved the church"[195] as we need to see how that works in practice. And we best see that by spending time with people who have learned to walk that truth day in and day out.

There is something that doesn't sit quite right with me when I observe church leaders who are occupied with the business of doing church and yet don't have the same value for spending time with people as was demonstrated by Jesus. If a pastor needs to be insulated or protected from the crowds of people in his congregation, might he perhaps be withholding the fruit of the vineyard from the landowner?

If you think about it, there isn't any need for evangelists in Heaven, since nobody there needs to be saved. And there probably isn't any need for teachers, since those

---

195 Ephesians 5:25

who have seen our Lord bear his likeness.[196] And what need is there for shepherds when the dwelling of God is among his people?

What then will we do in Heaven? I imagine that there will be a lot of time spent just being with Papa and his family. So, when we pray that the Kingdom should come on Earth as in Heaven, could it be that we are (among other things) praying for fellowship that is more being and less doing?

Redemptive relationships

When people crowded around Jesus, his response was always redemptive. He healed people, he blessed children, he encouraged and respected women, he touched those who were unclean, he spoke words of grace and compassion to people who were expecting condemnation and rejection.

When Jesus looked at a sinner, he did not see a rule-breaker so much as he saw a candidate for grace and redemption. The best example of this is the story of the woman who was brought before Jesus after having been caught in the act of adultery.[197]

It was the religious leaders who brought this woman to Jesus. They pushed her around and humiliated her, treating her as if she had no value. They quoted their rules, which said that she ought to be put to death, both in order to demonstrate their own external righteousness and in hope of trapping Jesus into either violating his own Law or his own nature.

---
196 1 John 3:2
197 John 8:1-11

But Jesus didn't argue or debate with these men. Neither did he accuse the woman. Instead, he began playing in the dirt. This surprising and unconventional response caught them off guard, so they pressed him again to pass a judgment.

The Bible doesn't tell us what Jesus wrote in the dirt, but it must have made some impact. Because when he later said something like, "Sure, you guys can kill her; just be sure that the first person to throw a stone has never broken any of the rules," they backed off. One by one, they realized that nobody would dare to make that claim about themselves. And so they wandered away leaving the woman crushed in fear, humiliation and disgrace. Jesus could have condemned her, but instead, spoke words of redemption: "You are not condemned. There is hope. Go and walk in freedom."

In every encounter between Jesus and some individual, it is clear that Jesus' goal was to communicate redemption. He didn't always cater to the person's wishes. Often, as with the woman at the well,[198] he looked beyond their expression of desire or discomfort in order to bring healing to the root issue that was keeping them from seeing into his Kingdom.

Clearly, releasing redemption is a big part of the fruit that brings pleasure to the landowner. But, if our lives never touch people in need of redemption or if we are quicker to communicate condemnation, distrust or apathy, then we are most certainly withholding fruit from the landowner.

Most of the times that the religious leaders of the day got indignant were cases where Jesus overlooked the

---

198 John 4:7-26

outward rules because he was looking to a redemptive purpose beyond those rules. For example, Jesus touched a leper, challenged a rich young man about his wealth, and healed on the sabbath.

Healing and deliverance

In fact, it looks as though Jesus healed everyone who came to him. One day, when a whole crowd of people had gathered, one of the religious leaders showed up and begged Jesus to come and heal his daughter who was lying on her deathbed. As they were on their way to his house, crowds of people pressed upon Jesus from all sides.

There was a woman in the crowd who suffered from an incurable bleeding sickness. In her desperation, she pushed her way through the crowd, thinking that if only she could touch his garment she would be healed. She did, and she was.

But immediately, her joy turned to apprehension, as Jesus stopped in his tracks and demanded to know who had touched him. She had good reason to be afraid. First, she had disturbed the great prophet who was busily on his way to carry out his business with the leader of the synagogue. In addition, she was a woman, and had willfully dared to touch a man who was not her father, brother or husband. Even worse, she had a discharge of blood and was ritually unclean, thereby making anyone she touched unclean as well. According to the rules, she deserved severe punishment for her brazen disrespect.

And yet, that was not why Jesus stopped. Rather, he knew that the woman had been physically healed. But that was not enough for Jesus. He also wanted to bless the woman for her courage and her faith. He wanted this "unclean, outcast woman" to hear that she was valuable and accepted. He called her daughter.[199]

This was not an isolated incident, but a typical example of Jesus touching not only the body but also the soul and spirit. A close look at the healings which are described in some detail in the gospels, shows that Jesus was after more than just meeting the person's physical need.

When Jesus healed a leper, he did so by reaching out and touching the man.[200] According to the rules, touching a leper was forbidden since it would make one unclean. The result was that a leper not only had a physical ailment, but also carried a huge burden of rejection. Jesus' touch was designed to bring healing to his soul as well as his body.

When Jesus healed a man born blind, he did so by spitting on the ground and making mud, which he then put on the man's eyes.[201] We may think that was an odd way to go about healing, but Jesus had a purpose. Just prior to this healing, Jesus had been asked whether it was the parents' sin or the man's own sin that was responsible for his blindness. In other words, the common assumption in that culture was that if a person had a defect then they were under a curse. And an accursed person has no value in society, so they end up being on the receiving end of cursing, spitting and other mistreatment. We can imagine that when this blind man heard Jesus spit, he figured he would once again be

---

199 Luke 8:48
200 Matthew 8:3
201 John 9:6

rejected and abused. But instead, Jesus turned this sound of disgrace into an instrument of healing.

Freedom of choice

After healing the man born blind, Jesus left him on his own. This wasn't to abandon the man, but rather to bring freedom. Never did Jesus use healing to manipulate or coerce people into following him. Neither did he reserve his goodness only for those who "deserved" it.

Jesus went about doing good things because he was demonstrating the nature of his Father. And Father God is really, really good. But when it came to the issue of following him, Jesus always spoke in terms of an invitation.

For example, when a young man came to Jesus and asked what he needed to do to gain eternal life, Jesus answered "If you want to be perfect..."[202] The man went away, saddened by the conditions Jesus had laid out for him. We don't know what the man did after he had time to think it all through. But we know that Jesus gave him the freedom to choose. Jesus didn't beg or go chasing after the young man. Neither did he change the conditions or make any effort to persuade the man to make the right choice.

Jesus' approach may seem a bit harsh, but the value of love is measured by the risk of losing it. If I am forced to follow someone, then there is no requirement for love. But if I am free to choose rejection, then choosing love has infinitely more value.

---

202 Matthew 19:21

When the landowner turned the vineyard over to his tenants, he went away. In other words, he gave them the freedom to run the vineyard as they saw fit. And consequently, they were also free to break their agreement with the landowner by refusing him the fruit of the vineyard.

In the same way, Jesus invited his disciples to follow him. But he also gave them the freedom to choose betrayal, and Judas made that choice. Jesus could have prevented the betrayal, either by not choosing Judas or by putting limitations on Judas so that the opportunity would not have arisen. But that kind of manipulation is not the way of our God.

Food for thought

What specific steps can you take to make your practice of Christianity more people-oriented? In your relationships with people, do you draw out the best in them? Are you a well of healing and restoration to the people around you? Are freedom, peace and rest among the words that people who know you would use to describe you and to describe how they feel when they are together with you?

The framework

When the landowner planted his vineyard, he walled it in, dug a winepress and set up a watchtower. The wall, winepress and watchtower are elements of a framework to make the vineyard fruitful and productive. They are practical and useful tools, but you can't drink a wall. The framework is not the fruit, and we need to be constantly on guard against letting the framework overshadow the fruit.

In the same manner, church structures, rituals and traditions are a framework. But they are not the fruit which the Father desires. As long as the framework contributes to strengthening and expanding the relationship between the Father and his children, they are a good thing. Just as a wall, a winepress and a watchtower are good and useful tools for wine production.

Occasionally, I have read articles or academic works that are written from the point of view that the Apostle Paul was out to create a religion. Some of these works have looked at the theology described in Paul's letters and how it differed from the Judaism of his day, or even from the teaching of Jesus. For the most part, such comments are written from the perspective of the institutionalized form of Christianity that is prevalent in our day. But I do not find this line of thinking to be consistent with Paul's own writings.

Paul was not out to build a religion. His motivation was to prepare a worthy bride for his beloved Jesus.[203] It seems to me that he gave little thought to structures beyond the personal relationships that arose in the fellowship of believers. He was not concerned about positions or titles,[204] neither his own nor the positions of others. It is not that Paul was opposed to structures, as long as they did not get in the way of preparing a pure and spotless bride.

---

203 2 Corinthians 11:2
204 See Galatians 2:6

The framework built by the landlord was built with the express purpose of making the vineyard fruitful and productive. So it is worth taking a closer look at how these structures contribute to preparing a worthy bride.

The wall

The purpose of a wall is to provide safety. A wall is designed to hold everything that would kill, steal and destroy away from the vineyard. A wall makes it possible for the vines to grow and develop without fear.

> *There is no fear in love. But perfect love drives out fear, because fear has to do with punishment. The one who fears is not made perfect in love. (1 John 4:18)*

As can be seen from this verse, the opposite of fear is perfect love. In practice perfect love is revealed in two manners: an understanding of identity and freedom from punishment. In a healthy congregation, both of these expressions of perfect love are within the domain of the shepherd. Without a shepherd, the sheep will feel harassed and helpless[205] rather than being at rest and producing good fruit.

The role of the shepherd is to care for and protect the sheep. Shepherding[206] is about meeting needs, healing hurts and providing nourishment. This is best

---

205 Matthew 9:36
206 The term shepherding, as I use it here, does not refer to the "shepherding movement" of the 1970's and 80's, but to the role of pastoral care. I choose the word shepherd rather than pastor because, in many churches, pastor is often the title of an employee whose gifting and responsibilities may not necessarily be shepherding.

accomplished by leading the sheep into a place of rest and safety – into a fundamental understanding of their identity as fully adopted and accepted children of the Great King.

As we grow in understanding of our royal identity, we see more clearly how valuable we are to the Lord. This allows us to rest in the knowledge that he is good and that he is always with us, providing for our safety.

Understanding our identity also frees us from the fear of punishment. Our identity as children of the King is a result of the fact that the entire punishment for our sins has already been paid. There is nothing that Jesus failed to take with him on the Cross, so there is nothing left to punish.

Another thing that can damage the wall and make us feel less safe is a poverty mentality. By this, I mean a culture of feeling and acting as though there are not enough resources to go around. There are a number of ways this can play out. Obviously, if a church leadership is very focused on getting people to give their time and or money to the business of doing church, then the result will not be a culture that makes people feel safe. If we look at newcomers to our fellowship primarily in terms of what resources they bring with them and how those could be tapped to meet our ministry needs, then it is a bit like the tenants who beat the messengers that were sent to them. If the underlying message in our congregation is that there aren't enough resources to go around, then we misrepresent the landlord who provides in abundance.

There are a number of ways that structures may be implemented in a congregation or fellowship of congregations. Shepherding roles may be filled by professionally trained staff or raised up through gifting and experience. The key is that the structure must contribute to the goal of making the sheep feel safe, free and loved. In this way, a richly fruitful crop will be made ready for the harvest.

The winepress

The winepress is an essential and unavoidable part of turning grapes into wine. But it can also be a messy and unpleasant process for the grapes themselves. This is the domain of the teacher.

Discipleship is the process of learning through the experience gained by following someone who has walked the road before you. Just as you cannot simply command a cluster of grapes to be wine, neither can you only instruct a person to maturity. The process takes time and requires transformation. Disciples are best produced when the wisdom, experience, maturity and character of the teacher rub off on the disciple.

> *As iron sharpens iron, so one person sharpens another. (Proverbs 27:17)*

Sermons, Sunday school classes and Bible studies will not automatically produce disciples, because the transfer of information does not of itself produce changed lives. What is needed are teachers who have themselves been so crushed by Jesus the cornerstone[207] that they naturally lead people to a transformation by the renewing of their minds. We don't need teachers who teach us to follow instructions so much as we need teachers who can

---

207 Matthew 21:44

demonstrate for us the nature of God in their own lives, in practical ways that we can learn to imitate.[208]

Just as you cannot make wine without crushing the grapes, so there are things in the life of the disciple that will need to be crushed. An important aspect of the winepress is to crush the grapes in such a way that they do not lose any of their sweetness. If the sweetness is lost, there will be no fermentation and the wine will never come to maturity.

This is one reason why the winepress is built inside of the wall. The process of crushing grapes must be carried out within a context of safety. It must not be done too brutally, and it is important to protect the grapes from contamination. In the same manner, the process of shepherding must create a culture and environment of safety so that the process of discipling can bring about the transformation necessary to produce maturity without damaging trust or harming identity.

The most pleasing disciples, like the best wines, will not be harsh or bitter. Neither will they leave a sour aftertaste. Rather there is a sweetness and a fragrance of Heaven.[209] If the winepress is not contributing to this kind of fruitfulness, then something definitely needs to be adjusted.

The watchtower

The watchtower gives perspective. It is from the watchtower that one may see what is coming,[210] be it

---

208 1 Corinthians 11:1
209 2 Corinthians 2:15
210 Habakkuk 2:1

weather or foes or the way of the wind. It is also the place of awaiting the arrival of the landowner. In other words, the watchtower represents the prophetic realm.

> *Where there is no revelation, people cast off restraint; but blessed is the one who heeds wisdom's instruction. (Proverbs 29:18)*

Revelation (or word from God, or vision, as other versions translate it) is an essential part of Kingdom of Heaven life. As this verse shows, there are dire consequences for a people which lacks revelation. Various Bible translations interpret these consequences differently, such as: cast off restraint, run wild, perish, are uncontrolled, are made naked, etc. There is no doubt that a people in such a condition is far from being the kind of fruit for which the landowner is looking.

The perspective gained from the watchtower plays an essential role in empowering the function of the wall. It is from the watchtower that one sees the impending danger from the storms or foes which may come to threaten the vineyard. It is vital that those in the watchtower are watching and prepared to keep the vineyard informed about what is coming. But if the message from the watchtower is not spoken with a heart of safety and protection, then the workers inside the wall might just fail to understand the message, thereby severely weakening the defense of the vineyard.

Likewise, the winepress is empowered to stay focused on its calling when those in the watchtower are faithfully keeping watch for the landowner. It is the role of the watchmen to seek after the landowner, to feel which direction the wind is blowing and to interpret what would bring the landowner pleasure. As this is communicated to the winepress, the necessary adjustments may be made so that the fruit of the vineyard will be even more pleasant.

It is also important for the those in the watchtower to discern between the two. If the lookout fails to understand the nature of the landlord, he can easily misrepresent the landlord. If we don't see him as an abundant provider, we might perceive him to be a thief. If we don't see him as a protector we might perceive him to be an attacker. If we don't receive him as a lover we end up rejecting him as an enemy.

Most certainly there was a failure in the watchtower which contributed to the tenants in the vineyard mistaking the landowner's servants (and son) for foes. Had those in the watchtower seen and understood which direction the landowner was moving, they would never have killed the son.

The wine

These three structural elements represent three of the five gifts of leadership described in Ephesians 4:11. And the fruit of these gifts, when functioning properly, is unity, maturity and walking in the fullness of Christ.

You may be wondering, what about the other two gifts (apostle and evangelist)? Though they do not as clearly or directly map to the structures built by the landowner in the parable, I believe that they are also important aspects of the framework that makes for a healthy congregation. So, I'll stretch the imagery a little bit further.

The apostolic gifting is kind of like the vineyard's production manager. It brings balance to the framework by helping to keep the focus on producing the best possible wine rather than over-prioritizing any one of the aspects of safety, discipleship or revelation to the detriment of the others. A true apostolic gifting will not only be concerned about making a good product in his own vineyard, but will also be passionate about producing good wine, both locally, regionally, nationally and globally. Like the friend of the bridegroom, who spends himself in every way possible to insure that the bride is ready and waiting when the bridegroom arrives, an apostle is attentive to the heart of the landowner and focused on seeing the landowner's goals met.

The evangelist is kind of like the salesman. The role of the salesman is to get people interested in the vineyard and its fruit. Of course, this can be done by telling people about the benefits of the wine, or about the sacrifices that have been made to create a good product, or about the details of how the vineyard goes about growing and harvesting their grapes and turning them into mature wine. But most vineyards use a more effective approach: wine tasting. In the same way, there is a lot to be said for the practice of demonstrating a hospitality that embraces people with warmth and joy, of generously and freely exercising the goodness of God, and of letting people become intoxicated by the sweetness of the love of Jesus. Where the fruit of the vineyard flows freely there will be joy and freedom and fellowship.

Leadership

The question remains as to how to build a fruitful framework. Or perhaps more relevant for most of us, how to remodel our existing framework to make it more suited to producing fruit that brings pleasure to the landowner.

The New Testament, as far as I can see, says very little specific and concrete about how churches and congregations should be structured. We can extract some examples from what was done by the believers of the day. But, I am not sure that these examples are meant to be taken as instructions or regulations for all congregations in all cultures in all times. Much of what we read in Acts and in the letters is about a bunch of believers experimenting to find out how to live the new Kingdom life into which they had stumbled.

But there are some guidelines, the most concrete being the guideline of building a leadership team. And yet, even this does not seem to be spelled out too rigidly. There are several verses that touch on the topic of a leadership team as a congregational structure.[211] There are some differences between how these verses touch on the subject, and there are also variations in how these verses have been translated into modern language.[212]

First of all, depending on the verse and/or the translation, these leaders are called elders, overseers or bishops. Second, being a leader may be described as an office (position) or simply an action (behavior). Third, a

---

211 Acts 14:23, Acts 20:17,28, 1 Timothy 3:1-7, 1 Timothy 5:17-19, Titus 1:5-9
212 Specifically, I've looked at the KJV, NIV, NCV, NASB and YLT translations.

leader might be appointed, elected, chosen, set down or ordained. Fourth, their activity could be to lead, rule or direct the affairs of the church. And they might have been selected or called out as leaders for an assembly, church, town or city.

That probably didn't help to make things any clearer.

I think that when looking at the question of structure, it is important to remember the context in which Paul and Luke wrote these passages. As previously mentioned, Paul was not focused on structure, offices or positions, but rather on producing good fruit. So when I read these verses, I tend to look upon the translations that imply structure (such as office and bishop) as having been influenced by an institutional church structure that did not exist until a couple hundred years after the text was first written.[213] In Paul's day, there were no Christian buildings and for the most part believers gathered informally (and often in secret) in homes.

So my own working understanding is that leaders were called elders because of their experience, that they were chosen by consensus in a group of believers to have a nurturing role of leading and caring for that fellowship. My understanding of servant leadership[214] leads me to believe that eldership was not so much an office but rather a result of character and experience which made it natural to be followed.

---

213 This does not mean that institutional structures are wrong, provided that they don't get in the way of producing fruit that brings pleasure to the landowner.
214 For example, see Mark 10:45

I believe that the best model we have for eldership is the model of parenting.[215] Just as parents are responsible for providing for the needs of their children while training them to maturity so that they may one day become parents themselves, the leaders of a congregation have a similar role of nurturing and training toward the goal of releasing a new generation of leaders. This is probably why Paul wrote[216] that an elder ought to have raised up believing children. If it doesn't work at home, you won't be able to make it work in the congregation.

The lists of qualifications in 1 Timothy 3 and Titus 1 are an illustration of the character that should be present in every mature believer. Fulfilling that list of requirements does not automatically make a person a leader. Rather, a person with a leadership gifting who does not demonstrate at least this level of character is not yet mature enough for a leadership role.

A healthy framework for the vineyard is developed by building a team of leaders who have the character and experience of elders and whose various giftings bring the breadth and balance to meet the various needs of producing good fruit. Such a framework will constantly have a priority of making that fruit ready and available to the landowner.

Food for thought

What specific steps can you take to contribute toward an increased atmosphere of safety in your congregation? What does it mean to you to rest? What does the goal of preserving sweetness in the process of discipleship mean to you? Do the

---

215 1 Corinthians 4:15
216 1 Timothy 3:4-5, Titus 1:6

visionary voices in your life lead you toward becoming more like a beautiful bride-to-be? Is the fruit of your life something that discerning people desire to taste?

The Kingdom

Just before Jesus ascended into Heaven, he had some final words with his disciples on a mountain top. They wanted to know if the time had come for them to take over the local government.[217] But Jesus said that their focus was all wrong. In Matthew's version of Jesus' final words[218], he made three key statements:

- Jesus has received all authority.
- Because of this, all nations should be taught his values.
- And, in order to enable us in that, Jesus is always with us.

The fact that Jesus has been given all authority establishes his position as Ruler and King. As a direct consequence of his rulership, he instructed his followers to go and make disciples of all nations. You might interpret this instruction to mean that they were to go out and evangelize so that some people from every nation would become believers. But the phrase actually means that every nation (or tribe or people group) is to be trained (discipled) to reflect the authority of Jesus. We'll come back to nations in the next section, but first we'll take a closer look at the concept of a kingdom.

As Jesus was on his way to Jerusalem before his crucifixion, he sent out 70 of his disciples as an advance team. He told them to bring peace and blessing to their

---

217 Acts 1:6
218 Matthew 28:18-20

hosts, to fellowship with them and meet their needs, and then to let them know that the Kingdom of God had come near.

But what, exactly, is this Kingdom? I have in my bookshelf a real treasure: a three-volume dictionary comprising nearly 5000 pages. This dictionary defines "kingdom" as follows:

> *The dominion or territory under the authority or rule of a king; the dominion of a king or monarch.*

And the next entry in this dictionary is for the phrase "Kingdom of Heaven, Kingdom of God":

> *A spiritual kingdom (Luke xvii. 21; John xviii. 36) which was "at hand" when John the Baptist announced the approaching advent of Jesus (Matt. iii. 2), and even after the ministry of the latter had commenced (Mark i. 15). The proper preparation for it was repentance (ibid.).* Jesus preached its coming (Luke iv. 43, viii. 1, xvi. 16). After His miraculous power had been experimentally demonstrated and the evangelists gone forth, it had arrived (Matt. xii. 28; Luke x. 11). It was to advance from small beginnings, like a seed which germinates, grows, and bears fruit (Mark iv. 26-32). Commencing on earth, its full establishment was to be at the conclusion of the present age in the other world (Matt. xii. 24 to 50; Luke xiii. 28, 29, xxii. 16,18). Before one could enter into the kingdom of God he must be born again (John iii. 3). The expression "kingdom of heaven" is the

common one in Matthew, while kingdom of God is frequent in Mark and Luke.[219]

That's a pretty big chunk of theology to find in a dictionary. But it demonstrates quite clearly that there is a big difference between this concept of the Kingdom of God and our natural understanding of a kingdom of this world. Jesus put it this way:

> *Once, on being asked by the Pharisees when the Kingdom of God would come, Jesus replied, "The coming of the Kingdom of God is not something that can be observed, nor will people say, 'Here it is,' or 'There it is,' because the Kingdom of God is in your midst." (Luke 17:20-21)*

At the time when Jesus walked the land, the territory of Israel was under the dominion and control of the Roman emperor. So, for the most part, the people of Israel were expecting that a Messiah would come and restore the kingdom by throwing off the foreign oppressors.

But what Jesus is saying here is that such an understanding is totally wrong, because his is a very different sort of Kingdom. The Kingdom of God is not a physical territory under the rule of a monarch. Just as the Father is spirit and those who would worship him must worship in spirit and truth[220] so his Kingdom is a spiritual kingdom.

The domain of his rule is primarily spiritual. By this I mean that the Kingdom operates to a large degree in realms that are not visible to the eye, that are not limited by time or space, and that are not dependent on being

---

[219] The American Encyclopædic Dictionary, Ogilvie Publishing Company, 1894
[220] John 4:24

physically connected with one another. In other words, rather than occupying some visible, definable, constrained area it permeates and influences the physical realm. For a natural kingdom to function, it needs to have boundaries, within which the authority of the ruler is at work. But the Kingdom of God has no such need for boundaries.

Jesus told a couple of parables to explain this:

> *And He said, "How shall we picture the kingdom of God, or by what parable shall we present it? "It is like a mustard seed, which, when sown upon the soil, though it is smaller than all the seeds that are upon the soil, yet when it is sown, it grows up and becomes larger than all the garden plants and forms large branches; so that the birds of the air can nest under its shade." (Mark 4:30-32 NASB)*

> *Again he asked, "What shall I compare the Kingdom of God to? It is like yeast that a woman took and mixed into about sixty pounds of flour until it worked all through the dough." (Luke 13:20-21)*

An understanding of a natural kingdom would look at this dough as the kingdom of bread. Here you have a large, well-mixed bread dough where all of the ingredients are working together to make a bunch of bread.

But Jesus says that hidden at strategic places throughout the bread dough are agents of change, that represent a different kind of Kingdom. They are not necessarily visibly different within the bread dough, but they have a calling and a destiny. They are there to cause that bread dough to rise up and become attractive, rather than just laying flat and heavy on the platter. Both before and during the baking process, the yeast pours out its breath (spirit), influencing and reshaping the bread for the better.

Or, in the case of the mustard seed, the Kingdom appears initially to be insignificant. But as it grows it provides shade. Shade, in the biblical context, implies shelter, pleasure and refreshment.[221] These are good things, which lift up a society and bring hope to the people.

When Jesus said, "I will build my church,"[222] he didn't actually say "church" as we understand it today. The Greek word used here, *ekklesia*, means "assembly" (literally, called out ones). At the time, the word had no religious connotation. In Jesus' day, it was used to describe a governing or influential body (or sometimes used to describe a crowd or mob[223]). The Romans used the term to describe the group of civic leaders whose assignment was to establish Roman culture in a conquered territory. In essence, Jesus was saying, "I will build up a body of cultural influencers whose calling is to bring the Kingdom of Heaven near."

The Kingdom of Heaven in you should influence the culture and society around you by working through that culture just as yeast is worked through a dough, and by bringing blessing just as a large plant provides shade. When the Kingdom culture flows in your heart then those who are near you come under that influence. Just as the purpose of yeast is to make the dough rise, so our purpose as Kingdom of Heaven citizens is not to take over the society in which we live, but rather to serve that

---

221 For example, see Psalm 91:1, Song 2:3 and Isaiah 32:2
222 Matthew 16:18
223 As in Acts 19:32, 39, 41

society with the goodness of God in such a way that society is lifted up to a better position.

This is a really important distinction. Most political leaders are concerned about power, both exercising their own power and all too often making sure that their opponents don't get any. But, in the Kingdom of Heaven, authority is gained not through exercising power but through submission.

Much of the opposition that the Kingdom of Heaven (in the form of the church) experiences in the political realm is a result of our political leaders' (all too frequently justified) fear that the church represents a natural kingdom which is out to throw off its rulers. To the degree that we, as Kingdom representatives, can disarm those fears we will experience a completely different reception in the halls of power.

This is what Paul was thinking when he wrote to Timothy about prayer "for kings and all those in authority, that we may live peaceful and quiet lives in all godliness and holiness."[224] We are not to look at political leaders (even ungodly ones, such as those who were leaders when Paul wrote these words) as enemies. Rather we should view them as people in need of our blessing so that they will use the keys that they hold in a manner that allows Kingdom of Heaven values to increase. Even those with whom we disagree should experience blessing when in our presence.

One person who understood this principle was the prophet Daniel. Daniel was the son of a nobleman in Jerusalem when that city was conquered by king Nebuchadnezzar. This king had destroyed his home,

---

224 1 Timothy 2:2

killed his parents, most likely made him a eunuch, and dragged him away to Babylon. He had every reason to dislike this king.

But Daniel had most likely read[225] the letter which the prophet Jeremaiah wrote to the exiles in Babylon. In it was written:

> *Seek the peace and prosperity of the city to which I have carried you into exile. Pray to the Lord for it, because if it prospers, you too will prosper. (Jeremiah 29:7)*

So Daniel served this king and several kings after him. He prayed for them and loved them and blessed them. Even when God prophesied judgment on his rulers, Daniel never carried an attitude of "now you're gonna get what you deserve." Rather, he said, "My lord, if only the dream applied to your enemies."

Daniel became a man of great influence through four political administrations. There is no record of his having any ambitions for a position of leadership. Rather, his lifestyle was one of worshiping the Lord and praying for the welfare of the city. And as a result, the wisdom that flowed from him carried him into a position of influence time and time again.

When Jesus warned his disciples to beware the yeast of the Pharisees, it was not because yeast is a bad thing. The problem was that the mindset of the Pharisees – their way of thinking and how it influenced society – was contrary to the culture of the Kingdom of Heaven. So Jesus was essentially saying to them, don't let that way of thinking influence you; rather, be an influence yourself.

---

225 See Daniel 9:2

Nations

It is especially important to have a Kingdom perspective when looking to the future. We are called to long for and to hasten[226] the return of our Lord. But that does not mean that we are to be looking forward to an increase of lawlessness. The degree to which we see the nations rage and stand in opposition to the Kingdom of God, is a measure of our failure to disciple those nations.

> *But when the Son of Man comes in His glory, and all the angels with Him, then He will sit on His glorious throne. All the nations will be gathered before Him; and He will separate them from one another, as the shepherd separates the sheep from the goats; and He will put the sheep on His right, and the goats on the left.*
>
> *Then the King will say to those on His right, "Come, you who are blessed of My Father, inherit the Kingdom prepared for you from the foundation of the world. For I was hungry, and you gave Me something to eat; I was thirsty, and you gave Me something to drink; I was a stranger, and you invited Me in; naked, and you clothed Me; I was sick, and you visited Me; I was in prison, and you came to Me."*
>
> *Then the righteous will answer Him, "Lord, when did we see You hungry, and feed You, or thirsty, and give You something to drink? And when did we see You a stranger, and invite You in, or naked, and clothe You? When did we see You sick, or in prison, and come to You?"*

---

226 2 Peter 3:12

> *The King will answer and say to them, "Truly I say to you, to the extent that you did it to one of these brothers of Mine, even the least of them, you did it to Me."*
>
> *Then He will also say to those on His left, "Depart from Me, accursed ones, into the eternal fire which has been prepared for the devil and his angels; for I was hungry, and you gave Me nothing to eat; I was thirsty, and you gave Me nothing to drink; I was a stranger, and you did not invite Me in; naked, and you did not clothe Me; sick, and in prison, and you did not visit Me."*
>
> *Then they themselves also will answer, "Lord, when did we see You hungry, or thirsty, or a stranger, or naked, or sick, or in prison, and did not take care of You?"*
>
> *Then He will answer them, "Truly I say to you, to the extent that you did not do it to one of the least of these, you did not do it to Me." These will go away into eternal punishment, but the righteous into eternal life. (Matthew 25:31-46 NASB)*

This parable is pretty straight-forward and doesn't need a lot of explanation. But I would like to point out one detail: the sheep and the goats represent *nations* rather than individual people. "All the nations will be gathered ... and he will separate them." The Greek word translated "them" simply refers to a previous noun, in this case "nations." So, although the parable definitely has applications for us as individuals, the primary object of this parable is actually nations.

The parable touches in particular on the concept of passing on the blessing.[227] The difference here between sheep nations and goat nations is closely tied to the degree to which those nations shared the blessings which they had received. We don't see a whole lot of that happening in the international political realm in our day. Rather, we see nations building physical, bureaucratic, and/or legal walls around themselves, in order to keep outsiders from gaining access to whatever blessings may be found inside the walls. Could it be that this goat-like behavior exists because we who represent the Kingdom of Heaven are failing to be salt and light in our nations?

Our calling as disciples of Jesus and citizens of his Kingdom is to disciple nations. Our calling as mustard seed in the garden is to be the shade of blessing and refreshment to our community. Our calling as yeast in the bread dough of this world is to cause the society in which we live to rise. Our challenge is to be a catalyst for change so that when the Son of Man comes in his glory, our nation will be found among the sheep on his right.

Food for thought

Are you mostly concerned about protecting your way of life from outside influence, or are you an agent of change in your own nation (and perhaps other nations, as well)? What can you do in your daily life to cause your city to rise? Are there community leaders whose lives you touch through your prayers and/or friendship?

---

227 See page 140

The Business of the Kingdom

One day, as Jesus was passing through Jericho, he invited himself to lunch at the home of a guy named Zacchaeus. This guy was unpopular, because he was a corrupt agent of the occupying powers. So folks in Jericho were astonished and a bit indignant that Jesus would want to be seen together with with such a person. But Jesus' acceptance led to a dramatic change in the heart and wallet of this outcast.

Jesus explained his actions by stating that he had come "to seek and save the lost." Or, as the NASB translation puts it, "to seek and save that which was lost." In this context, "the lost" encompasses more than just the lost souls of unbelievers. Jesus' mission wasn't only about the saving of lost souls, but also about bringing wholeness by redeeming culture, business and relationships that were placed under a curse when Adam and Eve first fell into sin.

And then...

> *While they were listening to these things, Jesus went on to tell a parable, because He was near Jerusalem, and they supposed that the kingdom of God was going to appear immediately. So He said, "A nobleman went to a distant country to receive a kingdom for himself, and then return. And he called ten of his slaves, and gave them ten minas and said to them, 'Do business with this until I come back.'*

"But his citizens hated him and sent a delegation after him, saying, 'We do not want this man to reign over us.'

"When he returned, after receiving the kingdom, he ordered that these slaves, to whom he had given the money, be called to him so that he might know what business they had done. The first appeared, saying, 'Master, your mina has made ten minas more.'

"And he said to him, 'Well done, good slave, because you have been faithful in a very little thing, you are to be in authority over ten cities.'

"The second came, saying, 'Your mina, master, has made five minas.' And he said to him also, 'And you are to be over five cities.'

"Another came, saying, 'Master, here is your mina, which I kept put away in a handkerchief; for I was afraid of you, because you are an exacting man; you take up what you did not lay down and reap what you did not sow.'

"He said to him, 'By your own words I will judge you, you worthless slave. Did you know that I am an exacting man, taking up what I did not lay down and reaping what I did not sow? Then why did you not put my money in the bank, and having come, I would have collected it with interest?'

"Then he said to the bystanders, 'Take the mina away from him and give it to the one who has the ten minas.' And they said to him, 'Master, he has ten minas already.' I tell you that to everyone who has, more shall be given, but from the one who *does not have, even what he does have shall be taken away. But these enemies of mine, who did not want me to reign over them, bring them here and slay them in my presence." (Luke 19:11-27 NASB)*

Jesus told this story because the people were hoping that the Kingdom of God would appear when he came to Jerusalem. With this parable, he was showing that the Kingdom would neither show itself in the way they expected nor with the timing they hoped for.

Doing business

The story starts out with a ruler who, before coming into the fullness of his rule, needed first to visit a distant country. In his absence, this ruler equipped his slaves with the resources they would need and instructed them to invest these resources in a way that would further his interests and his dominion.

In other words, the kingdom has been left in the hands of the servants, who have been fully equipped with the resources necessary for the kingdom to prosper, while awaiting the return of the king. The challenge is that the extent to which the kingdom actually does prosper in the absence of the king is directly related to what the servants do with those resources.

Of course, one aspect of the business of prospering the Kingdom of God has to do with bringing people to an encounter with the goodness of God which leads them to salvation, deliverance and freedom. But prospering the Kingdom is not restricted only to bringing salvation to lost souls.

Prospering the Kingdom of God also encompasses redeeming society: putting an end to the destruction and oppression of the devil, eradicating injustice and exploitation, making way for peace and reconciliation in relationships, and so on.

So these ten servants had been equipped and turned loose to do what they saw fit. Their instructions were to put the resources to work until the return of the ruler. But rather than being told exactly what to do, they were released to use their own creativity and ingenuity in an atmosphere of freedom.

The business of the kingdom works best in an atmosphere of freedom, which opens for a world of creativity in expressing that business. The king does not appear to have been so concerned with how his business was done, as long as his servants invested the resources entrusted to them with the goal of furthering their master's interests. But it is the nature of investment that there is always an element of risk involved. Typically, the greater potential return on an investment the greater the risk as well.

In an atmosphere of freedom, there is always room for making mistakes. Making a mistake is not sin. It is part of the process of learning to hear the heartbeat of the king. We do not punish children for falling down when they are learning to walk, or for misunderstanding when they are learning language. But the child who does not try to walk or speak is not living out their potential. In the same way, there is room for making mistakes in the business of the kingdom.

In the parable of the talents (recorded by Matthew), it says that each servant was given resources according to their ability.[228] I interpret this as each servant having been given appropriate resources for them to succeed within the sphere of their own gifting, talent and aptitude. It is not as though a blacksmith was expected to run a dairy, or a dancer expected to build houses. But a blacksmith would be expected to do his work in such a way that his business prospered honestly and his city was supplied with useful and dependable tools.

It is also apparent that each servant was given at least enough resources to succeed. Again, in the parable of the talents, the servants were given different amounts of resources, but each appears to have been given enough, according to their ability. There is no indication that those servants who prospered looked first at what they had been given with an attitude of, "I don't have enough here, how can I ever succeed?" Rather, there is every reason to believe that their master was a generous provider.

It is the nature of our King to give generously. He does not give gifts to his people based on whether or not we deserve them, but in accordance with his generous nature.[229] (After all, it is not a gift, that which is paid out as recompense for our deeds.) Our King gives his gifts according to the potential he sees in us. Which usually means that he gives enough for us to excel, while at the same time leaving it up to us to choose to excel (or to fail, if we so choose).

---

228 Matthew 25:15. Although there are many similarities between the parable of the minas and the parable of the talents, they were told on two different occasions and there are subtle differences both in purpose and in detail.
229 See Romans 12:6, Ephesians 4:7-8, Hebrews 2:4

In his final speech to the children of Israel, Moses said something interesting:

> *For the Lord your God is bringing you into a good land—a land with brooks, streams, and deep springs gushing out into the valleys and hills; a land with wheat and barley, vines and fig trees, pomegranates, olive oil and honey; a land where bread will not be scarce and you will lack nothing; a land where the rocks are iron and you can dig copper out of the hills. (Deuteronomy 8:7-9)*

In other words, the people were on their way to a land of abundant resources. But these resources would still need to be worked to create value and build a nation. They could choose to leave the iron and copper in the hills, or they could use the iron and copper to create useful items and works of art. The future health and wealth of the nation was entirely dependent on whether they chose to do business with the resources they were given, or instead resigned themselves to let the resources lie where they were. And, of course, the degree to which they (both individually and as a nation) would prosper was directly related to how well they went about their business.

Sadly, in the parable, there was one servant who allowed fear to so overwhelm him that he lost sight of his master's true nature. I believe it was not so much his failure to achieve a good return on investment as it was his fear-driven behavior that inflamed the wrath of his master. This fear not only caused him to misrepresent and slander the nature of his master, but it also paralyzed him from even the simple action of putting the investment on deposit in the bank.

Most likely, this servant understood and was in agreement with his master's goals. There is no indication that he was in opposition to the rule of his master or to the things which would further his master's interests in the kingdom. But, in his fear for how things would play out at the return of his master, he hid away the resources which had been entrusted to him rather than investing them in the kingdom of his master.

There are some in the church today who are in a similar position. With too great a focus on prophecies about the end of the age, the great tribulation, the reign of the antichrist, and such stuff, fear can easily overwhelm. If you see the world going into a downward spiral, you will most likely not prioritize investing resources in a way that enables the Kingdom of God to penetrate society,[230] but will rather hide those resources away inside the walls of the church so as not to be stained by the world outside.

Those who would curl up in an out-of-the-way place and wait for the return of the King may find his return to be more unpleasant than they had expected. The prophet Amos[231] warned that the day of the Lord would be a surprisingly terrible experience for those who, while awaiting that day focused on religious practice without prioritizing justice and righteousness in the society around them.

One day, when Jesus was out walking with his disciples, they came upon a man who had been born blind. The disciples, based on their understanding that a blind person was under a curse,[232] asked Jesus whether it was

---

230 Revelation 11:15
231 Amos 5:18-24
232 Deuteronomy 28:28

the sin of the parents or of the man himself that had caused him to be born blind. Jesus answered that this was no cause-and-effect relationship such as they supposed, but rather that the blindness was an opportunity for the works of God to be displayed. And then he said:

> As long as it is day, we must do the works of him who sent me. Night is coming, when no one can work. While I am in the world, I am the light of the world. (John 9:4-5)

On another occasion, he taught his disciples to pray that the Kingdom of Heaven would come to Earth and operate just as it does in Heaven.[233] There is more to prayer than just asking God to do stuff for us. Prayer is communication with God – a two-way dialog (if we take the time to listen). So a big part of praying for the Kingdom to come is about gaining the Lord's perspective on what that means.

Jesus said that we must do the works of the Kingdom while there is light in the world. And he said that he is that light. He also said that we (in whom he lives) are that light,[234] and we should let that light shine through the works we do so that people would be attracted to the Kingdom of Heaven.

Our calling is to put the resources we have been given to work, serving our community so that the culture of the Kingdom of Heaven permeates society.

---

233 Matthew 6:10
234 Matthew 5:14-16

Food for thought

Do you have enough? Do you let fear frame the way you invest in the future? If you are not currently going about "the business of the Kingdom," what can you start doing? If you are, then what can you do to increase the return on your investment?

Wealth

You may have noticed that the servants in this parable were put to work with resources that were not their own. They were not only instructed to do the work of prospering the kingdom, but they were also given the resources necessary to do that work, each according to his ability.

Likewise, the work of prospering the Kingdom of God is to be done with the King's resources. We are not called to do our best for God – working to build his Kingdom through our own strength and with our own resources. Rather, we are called to be filled with him – his nature, his Kingdom values, and most of all his Spirit – and let that life flow through us.

> *Jesus told his disciples: "There was a rich man whose manager was accused of wasting his possessions. So he called him in and asked him, 'What is this I hear about you? Give an account of your management, because you cannot be manager any longer.'*
>
> *"The manager said to himself, 'What shall I do now? My master is taking away my job. I'm not strong enough to dig, and I'm ashamed to beg—I*

know what I'll do so that, when I lose my job here, people will welcome me into their houses.'

"So he called in each one of his master's debtors. He asked the first, 'How much do you owe my master?'

" 'Nine hundred gallons of olive oil,' he replied.

"The manager told him, 'Take your bill, sit down quickly, and make it four hundred and fifty.'

"Then he asked the second, 'And how much do you owe?'

" 'A thousand bushels of wheat,' he replied.

"He told him, 'Take your bill and make it eight hundred.'

"The master commended the dishonest manager because he had acted shrewdly. For the people of this world are more shrewd in dealing with their own kind than are the people of the light. I tell you, use worldly wealth to gain friends for yourselves, so that when it is gone, you will be welcomed into eternal dwellings.

"Whoever can be trusted with very little can also be trusted with much, and whoever is dishonest with very little will also be dishonest with much. So if you have not been trustworthy in handling worldly wealth, who will trust you with true riches? And if you have not been trustworthy with someone else's property, who will give you property of your own?

"No one can serve two masters. Either you will hate the one and love the other, or you will be

> *devoted to the one and despise the other. You cannot serve both God and money."*
>
> *The Pharisees, who loved money, heard all this and were sneering at Jesus. He said to them, "You are the ones who justify yourselves in the eyes of others, but God knows your hearts. What people value highly is detestable in God's sight. (Luke 16:1-15)*

I have often found this parable to be a bit puzzling. At first glance, it looks as though Jesus is giving some sort of approval to dishonest behavior. But I do not believe that is the case.

The starting point of this story is a manager who has not been faithful in managing his master's resources. Since he knows full well that he is about to lose his job, he uses his last opportunity as manager to insure that he will still have friends in the community even after his job is gone.

Jesus' point here is not about dishonesty, but about "using worldly wealth to gain friends for yourselves, so that when it is gone, you will be welcomed into eternal dwellings." In other words, he is encouraging us to manage the resources that come under our influence in a way that will further the interests of the Kingdom of God.

But, what does that look like?

One approach is to simply do excellent work. We'll look at that in more detail in the next section. On a larger scale, it is about having a Kingdom perspective in all that you do, so that in every situation you see opportunities to make use of the resources around you in a way that will further the interests of the Kingdom of God.

For example, a teacher might declare that peace and truth shall prevail in their classroom, thereby denying lying, cheating or fighting spirits the opportunity to operate when school is in session. Though a teacher does not own the classroom, they can still exercise their authority as the teacher in that classroom and use that resource for the furtherance of the Kingdom.

Or it might be a store clerk who takes the opportunity to speak words of blessing over each customer that passes through. Or an engineer who designs more safety into a system than might strictly be necessary.

These are but a few simple examples of how ordinary people can make use of resources which are not their own to express Kingdom values and bring blessing.

At the same time, Jesus' next statement is equally important: you must steward the resources that you manage in a trustworthy manner. Unlike the manager in this parable, who dishonestly used his master's resources for his own benefit, when furthering the Kingdom of Heaven with the resources we manage it must be done in a way that also brings blessing to the owner of the resources.

A store clerk who ignores their customers because he is too focused on some single aspect of furthering the Kingdom will most likely not be viewed as trustworthy by his boss.

Jesus also said that unfaithfulness with someone else's property will prevent you from obtaining property of your own. The prophet Malachi says this in another way when he refers to failing to give tithes and offerings as stealing God's property.[235] This might explain why there are some Christians who struggle with financial lack.[236] If they are not trustworthy with God's share, who will give them abundance of their own?

So, the principle we extract from the parable of the dishonest manager is to do business with the resources that come under our influence in a way that furthers the interests of the Kingdom of Heaven while still bringing blessing and honor to the owner of those resources. Now, let's plug that back into the parable of the minas.

One of the servants had been given one mina and had put it to work. On his master's return, that investment had multiplied to ten more minas. He came before his master joyfully, knowing that he had been a good steward of that which had been entrusted to him. But imagine his surprise when the master rewarded his faithfulness by making him the governor of ten cities!

Another servant, perhaps bound by his own love of money, had fearfully guarded that mina which was not his own. But he did not manage it faithfully. To the surprise of all, the master took away this mina and gave it to the servant who had earned ten.

---

235 Malachi 3:8-12. Perhaps you think that tithing is an Old Testament concept which does not apply in our day since we are no longer under the Law. I won't argue that point. I will just say that I have experienced a lot of blessing in my life through faithfully tithing and giving generously.

236 I do not mean to imply that this is the only source of financial lack. There is a lot of oppression and destruction in the world, and many are victims of things far beyond their control. But even in these circumstances, faithfulness with small things and faithfulness with that which is not yours releases blessing.

He who has shown himself trustworthy with little (with restricted resources and limited expectations and little likelihood of being noticed) has demonstrated that he has the strength of character to be trusted with much more. And perhaps even more importantly, he who can not be trusted to manage even a small amount of worldly resources well will not be entrusted with true (spiritual) riches.

So the first servant, now the governor of ten cities, has eleven minas. Why? I believe it is because this servant has demonstrated that he will invest the resources in his possession in a manner that will continue blessing, prospering and advancing the kingdom. He is not likely to just sit on the capital or to use it dishonestly, because his character has been tested and proven.

That servant had been given one mina by his master. While his master was away, he invested the mina (which was not his own) and earned ten more. When the master returned, he reclaimed his one mina but let the servant keep the ten which he had earned (plus the one mina given to him from the other servant). Armed with this wealth, he was then entrusted to govern ten cities.

Both of the servants who were set to govern cities had come with the same report to their master: "your wealth has produced more wealth." By this they were not promoting themselves, but they were saying that they had begun to understand how to use worldly wealth in a way that gains eternal friendship, and how to faithfully handle wealth which was not their own.

The unfaithful servant had hoarded the mina given to him. Rather than putting the money to work, as he had been instructed, he hid the money away. His own words show that his actions were driven by fear. He believed that this hoarded wealth would save him from what he feared, the wrath of his master. But he was completely wrong.

What can be seen here is that Kingdom of God economics is different from the economic systems of this world. Where capitalism is about hoarding wealth, socialism is about forcibly redistributing wealth and communism is about centralized control of wealth, Kingdom economics is about using wealth to be a blessing.

> *Beloved, I pray that in all respects you may prosper and be in good health, just as your soul prospers. (3 John 2 NASB)*

It is not a sin to prosper. The first servant was not only allowed to keep his earnings, but he was rewarded in multiple ways for his faithfulness. And that faithfulness was closely tied to his generating wealth. But the wealth did not own him. He had proved himself faithful in a small thing (doing the business of his master) and could therefore be trusted to govern ten cities.

In the Kingdom of Heaven, ownership is a "lightweight" concept. By this I mean that we should hold the things we own with an open hand. We do not own things in order to have them, we own things in order to share them. A careful look at the way the first century church handled ownership[237] shows this. It was not that the believers stopped owning things, but that they held their wealth lightly – releasing wealth at the right time to bring blessing. They did not all move into poverty, nor did they turn all of their possessions over to the church leaders to manage. They still had homes in which to

---

237 See Acts 2:44-45, 4:32-37, 5:1-4

gather.[238] But they looked upon their possessions as blessings to be shared.

Through the years I have had numerous positions of leadership, both within the church and in other settings. A leader frequently has to act as an owner, be it as a board member or elected representative or investor or whatever. I have found that, for many people, ownership ends up being a lot about control.

For example, a board of directors will frequently be concerned about making sure that the business or activity is run the way the board desires. If the board is unhappy, then heads may roll (so to speak). All too often, members in a volunteer organization will just up and leave if things aren't happening the way they wish them to be done. Even a missions board can find itself putting undue pressure on their missionaries through their performance expectations or budget decisions.

But the Kingdom of God does not operate like that. I have had the pleasure in recent years of participating in a form of ownership that functions in a very different manner. When I first began to understand what I had stumbled into, I was overwhelmed with joy. It turned out that all of us who were representing ownership in this activity were there with the philosophy of "we are here to bring resources so that the vision-bearers of this activity will be able to live out their dreams, and know that we stand behind them."

That experience has changed how I look at ownership, and it influences how I act as a leader. I no longer participate in leadership with the goal of seeing things

---

238 Acts 12:12. This is probably 5-10 years after the incident in Acts 5:1-4.

happen my way. Rather, I go into it thinking, "what resources can I bring so that the key players will succeed in bringing their vision to fruition?"

Food for thought

Are you able to look at wealth with a Kingdom perspective? Can you be trusted with "true riches"? What specific steps can you take to hold your possessions more lightly? Is your understanding of ownership more influenced by control or by freedom and generosity?

Excellence

Jesus told yet another parable about working:

> *Suppose one of you has a servant plowing or looking after the sheep. Will he say to the servant when he comes in from the field, "Come along now and sit down to eat"? Won't he rather say, "Prepare my supper, get yourself ready and wait on me while I eat and drink; after that you may eat and drink"? Will he thank the servant because he did what he was told to do? So you also, when you have done everything you were told to do, should say, "We are unworthy servants; we have only done our duty." (Luke 17:7-10)*

The point of this parable is quite simple: There is nothing particularly commendable about a servant doing everything that they are expected to do. It is only in going beyond expectations that we move into the realm of excellence.

One way to look at this is by thinking of a number line.[239] At one end you could have -100, which represents total evil (a worshiper of the demonic, or the instigator of genocide, or something similarly abominable). At the other end would be +100, which represents total good (however difficult it may be to picture that in a human). At the zero mark you have the servant who has done everything that was expected of them, but nothing more.

So what is the point? Well, if doing the business of the Kingdom involves investing resources to cause Kingdom of God culture to influence the society in which we live, then we would probably like that investment to return more than zero.

In most communities there are very few people, if any, that are close to the -100 point on the number line. Most people are relatively law-abiding (at least enough to not get caught). They may sometimes drive faster than the speed limit, tell the occasional dirty joke, and perhaps cheat just a little bit on their taxes. But they probably think of themselves as pretty good, since they aren't all that bad. These people would typically be somewhere between -10 and -5.

But in the Kingdom of God, doing *everything* that is expected of you only gets you to zero. In order to balance all of the people on the minus side, we need to make investments of excellence.

Using linear mathematics, it would take a hundred people at +100 to compensate for a thousand of the people at -10 in our community. That's not a very hope-inspiring equation. Fortunately, Kingdom of God math

---

[239] Thanks to Arthur Burk, whose teaching first introduced this number line concept to me.

works differently. For people walking on the plus side of the number line, "five of you will chase a hundred, and a hundred of you will chase ten thousand."[240] Did you notice that with this kind of math, five people could chase 20 each, while a hundred people could chase 100 each? In other words, as the Kingdom of God increases its influence in society, the impact of that influence increases even more.

By now, you might be thinking, "Hey, wait just a minute here. I am saved by grace, and not by works!" And that is entirely true. All of your sins and failures – past, present and future – are covered by the blood of Jesus that was poured out from the Cross, and there is nothing you can do to change that. If Jesus is your Lord and Savior, then you *are* a son or daughter of God, and nothing that you do or refrain from doing will change your position in Christ for the better or for the worse.

The number line concept is not about your salvation or your identity. Rather, it is about being enough of a heavyweight to tip the balance in your community. It is about discipling nations so that they are found among the sheep rather than among the goats. It is about investing the minas we have been entrusted, rather than hiding them away.

The greatest hindrance to changing the spiritual climate of a community is not the unbelieving population (regardless of how far on the minus side they may be found). Rather, it is those believers who are complacent in the grace which they have received, and yet are still walking on the minus side.

---

240 Leviticus 26:8

It all comes down to walking in excellence. And I believe that the road to excellence is not so much found in trying to be excellent as it is in gaining spiritual weight.

One of the easiest ways to become a heavyweight in the natural realm is to eat a lot of fast food and always choose to supersize the portions. Now, if the Lord is your portion,[241] how often do you ask him to supersize it?

Jesus said that unless you eat his flesh and drink his blood, you will be without life.[242] The Psalmist spoke of being satisfied with the richest of foods[243] and said, "Taste and see that the Lord is good."[244] And King David, in Psalm 23, described himself as likened to a sheep laying down in a green pasture. Sheep don't usually lie down in a lush pasture until they have eaten their fill.

Perhaps there is a clue about this in the parable of the servant. After the servant came in from working the fields, he would be expected to feed his master before feeding himself. If we come to our Lord bringing him the richness of foods that satisfy him, then how can he who so loves us fail to respond in like kind?

I believe that, in this context, the richest of foods that we can prepare and serve to our Lord is worship in spirit and truth. This kind of worship would take the form of expressions of thanksgiving, praise and adoration in an atmosphere of rest and intimacy. A good meal is not to be wolfed down in a hurry so you can be done with it. Rather, it should be savored and enjoyed. And, as the Lord finds a place of rest in our presence, then he will

---

241 Psalm 16:5-6
242 John 6:53
243 Psalm 63:5
244 Psalm 34:8

accept the invitation to come over us with all of his weight.

It is out of this position of rest that excellence finds a place to grow. Several years ago, my wife and I found that the time had come for us to move to a different fellowship of believers. We had been faithful members of a congregation with a "servant personality" and had through the years given ourselves to many of the activities there. The leaders in our new congregation recognized that we were tired and gave us room to just be at rest as a part of the fellowship. It was not long before we made a profound discovery: we were actually more fruitful just being ourselves than when we had been "doing ministry."

When we meet the Lord in that place of rest and allow him to fill us with the richness of his delicious goodness, then we grow fat on his nature. The more we gaze upon him, the more like him we become. And that likeness with our Father translates into excellence projected upon our surroundings. His faithfulness leads us to be good and faithful employees or employers. His creative nature flowing through us will inspire creativity and ingenuity in our work. His wisdom will give us insight in meeting the challenges and solving the problems that meet us in the workplace and in our daily lives. He will inspire us to do things which are not our responsibility but are a source of blessing, such as picking up someone else's litter or paying for someone else's groceries.

The prophet Zechariah once had a vision that touches on this:

> *Then I looked up, and there before me were four horns. I asked the angel who was speaking to me, "What are these?"*
>
> *He answered me, "These are the horns that scattered Judah, Israel and Jerusalem."*
>
> *Then the Lord showed me four craftsmen. I asked, "What are these coming to do?"*
>
> *He answered, "These are the horns that scattered Judah so that no one could raise their head, but the craftsmen have come to terrify them and throw down these horns of the nations who lifted up their horns against the land of Judah to scatter its people."*
>
> *Then I looked up, and there before me was a man with a measuring line in his hand. I asked, "Where are you going?"*
>
> *He answered me, "To measure Jerusalem, to find out how wide and how long it is."*
>
> *While the angel who was speaking to me was leaving, another angel came to meet him and said to him: "Run, tell that young man, 'Jerusalem will be a city without walls because of the great number of people and animals in it. And I myself will be a wall of fire around it,' declares the Lord, 'and I will be its glory within.' " (Zechariah 1:18-2:5)*

First, Zechariah sees four "horns." These horns, which scatter the people and depress them so that they are unable to raise their heads, symbolize oppressive spirits.

Next, he sees four craftsmen. A craftsman is a skilled worker or artisan. The prime example of a biblical craftsman is Bezalel, the first person in the Bible who is described as being filled with the Spirit of God.[245]

These craftsmen were coming to *terrify* the horns. The implication is that when people do their work skillfully under the influence of the Spirit of God, this terrifies those spirits which oppress a community and causes them to lose their grip on the land.

And what happened next? Zechariah saw an angel measuring the dimensions of the city. Why? Because the Lord was taking inventory. He was calculating the supply of resources to release for the restoration of the city.

It is really quite simple: When you walk in the realm of excellence, the result is fear in the camp of the enemy and a release of heavenly resources for restoration.[246]

Food for thought

What are two specific "beyond expectations" things that you can start doing in your daily life to increase your leverage on the number line of your community? How can you go about increasing your appetite for the rich foods of excellence?

Cities

The theme of restoration, and of restoring cities in particular, runs throughout the Bible. The first city was built by Cain, after he had murdered his brother Abel and

---

245 See Exodus 31:2-5, 35:30-35
246 Thanks to Eric Johnson, whose teaching introduced me to this interpretation of Zechariah's vision.

then withdrawn from the presence of the Lord.²⁴⁷ And the final scenes of the book of Revelation depict a city coming down as a bride adorned for her husband. In between these two extremes there is room for a lot of restoration, both of individual cities and of the whole concept of a city.

The consequences of the fall of man took root very quickly, and Cain became the first person recorded in the Bible to take on the full nature of the serpent which had deceived his parents. Cain became a murderer, in the likeness of the devil (who was a murderer from the beginning²⁴⁸). The curse that fell upon Cain as a consequence of this murder was that he would be a restless wanderer. But before long, perhaps in a futile attempt to escape the curse, he built a city.

The nature of the builder of the first city has been implanted in the entire concept of the city: murder, restlessness and the futile attempts of mankind to escape the curse through their own strength. Oswald Chambers put it like this:

> *The first civilization was founded by a murderer, and the whole basis of civilized life is a vast, complicated, more or less gilded-over system of murder. We find it more conducive to human welfare not to murder men outright, we do it by a system of competition.*²⁴⁹

---

247 Genesis 4:12-17
248 John 8:44
249 Chambers, Oswald, *Our Portrait in Genesis*, Oswald Chambers Publications Association, 1957, page 15.

As Noah left the ark, God blessed Noah and said, "Be fruitful and increase in number and fill the Earth."[250] But it didn't take long before men chose to oppose this blessing by building a city rather than filling the Earth.[251] This brought an element of rebellion into the concept of the city. And God responded by confusing the language of men.

Though this picture may look bleak, Jesus is looking forward to a pure and spotless bride in the form of a city.[252] In this city there will be no death, homelessness or curse.[253] All of the evil that was implanted in human civilization from its establishment by Cain will be restored to the Creator's original intent.

Although the restoration of the city will find its complete fulfillment in the new Heaven and Earth of the next age, I believe that the process of restoration is at work throughout this age as well. For the government of our Lord is always on the increase.[254]

The first clear step toward restoring the concept of the city was the cities of refuge that were established when the nation of Israel came into their promised land. These cities were designated as places where a murderer could seek refuge and perhaps find deliverance from the punishment that was their due by the Law.[255] It may seem odd that God uses a structure originally established by a murderer as a tool for setting murderers free. But this is

---

250 Genesis 9:1
251 Genesis 11:4
252 Revelation 21:2, 9-10
253 Revelation 21:3-4, 22:3
254 Isaiah 9:7
255 Numbers 35:6-15, Deuteronomy 19:1-10

consistent with Kingdom thinking – strongholds of evil are broken by moving in the opposite spirit.

The next step has to do with rebuilding walls. For a city, walls signify safety. Within the walls one would expect to find community, while danger, fear and worry are prevented from entering.

> *The Spirit of the Sovereign Lord is on me, because the Lord has anointed me to preach good news to the poor. He has sent me to bind up the brokenhearted, to proclaim freedom for the captives and release from darkness for the prisoners, to proclaim the year of the Lord's favor and the day of vengeance of our God, to comfort all who mourn, and provide for those who grieve in Zion—to bestow on them a crown of beauty instead of ashes, the oil of gladness instead of mourning, and a garment of praise instead of a spirit of despair. They will be called oaks of righteousness, a planting of the Lord for the display of his splendor. They will rebuild the ancient ruins and restore the places long devastated; they will renew the ruined cities that have been devastated for generations. (Isaiah 61:1-4)*

This is the calling upon the Lord Jesus. He was anointed with the Holy Spirit to release a company of prisoners from their captivity. And then, those whom he set free would become rebuilders. We who are recipients of his saving grace, who are called oaks of righteousness, are the ones who carry the grace to renew ruined cities.

A parallel passage from Isaiah 58 puts this calling into a cause-and-effect relationship. Restoration of the city is firmly tied to deliverance from oppression.

> *If you do away with the yoke of oppression, with the pointing of the finger and malicious talk, and if you spend yourselves on behalf of the hungry and satisfy the needs of the oppressed, then your light will rise in the darkness, and your night will become like the noonday. The Lord will guide you always; he will satisfy your needs in a sun-scorched land and will strengthen your frame. You will be like a well-watered garden, like a spring whose waters never fail. Your people will rebuild the ancient ruins and will raise up the age-old foundations; you will be called Repairer of Broken Walls, Restorer of Streets with Dwellings. (Isaiah 58:9b-12)*

The first consequence of putting an end to oppression is that your light will become intensely bright. Or as Jesus put it:

> *You are the light of the world. A city on a hill cannot be hidden. ... In the same way, let your light shine before men that they may see your good deeds and praise your Father in Heaven. (Matthew 5:14,16)*

This is about eliminating darkness. In physics, darkness is the absence of light. Darkness is not in itself a quantity. You can't measure it or produce it. You can't "dark." A light can shine, but darkness can't "unshine." The same is true spiritually. Spiritual darkness is nothing more than that state which arises when we who are light are not shining. And one key to shining brightly is through delivering captives and eliminating oppression. This is what raises a city up from the depths, as it were, and sets it on a hill.

The business of restoration brings blessing on both those who are being restored and on the restorer: If you satisfy the needs of the oppressed ... the Lord will satisfy your needs. If you spend yourself on behalf of the hungry ... you will be like a spring whose waters never fail. If you do away with the yoke of oppression ... the Lord will strengthen your frame. Do you see the pattern here? It is in the use of resources and blessing to bring restoration and freedom that those resources increase!

Looking back now to the parable of the minas, each servant was given a measure of wealth and instructed to use that wealth in a manner that would further the interests of their master. Those servants who demonstrated the faithfulness to multiply what had been entrusted to them were promoted to governing cities.

Isaiah 58 and 61 demonstrate clearly that the interests of our Lord are firmly planted in deliverance and restoration. The resources he has given us include a crown of beauty, the oil of gladness and a garment of praise. These are things we are to invest in renewing the communities in which we live. As we prove ourselves faithful in these small things, we will gain authority and see the government of the Kingdom of Heaven increase in our cities. And as we do this work with excellence, we will see the resources of Heaven released in increasing measure for the rebuilding of the walls of peace and prosperity.

What does this look like? It starts with an anointing for blessing.

Hezekiah was a king who failed to see this. Through the first part of his reign, Hezekiah led a great revival in his nation, bringing both spiritual and material restoration to his kingdom. At one point he became deathly ill, but in answer to his prayers God healed him and gave him a miraculous sign. Sadly, the revival of Hezekiah's day did not carry into the next generation. In fact, his son Manasseh became perhaps the most evil king in the history of the nation. Why? Because Hezekiah gave no return for the benefit he had received.[256] Like the one servant, he hid away the blessings bestowed upon him for his own use in his own generation, rather than investing them in the purposes of his Lord.

Food for thought

To what extent are oppression, accusation and poverty in your community issues that touch you personally? What specific step can you take this week to start changing those patterns?

Promotion

The servant whose investment returned ten-fold was promoted to governing ten cities. This must have come as a shock to the servant. He was, in his own view, only doing what was expected of him. But his master saw more deeply. This was a servant whose gaze was fixed on his master, who understood his master's heart and who worked faithfully and diligently to further the interests of his master.

Although nothing in the story leads us to believe that the servant had set his ambitions on becoming a governor, it is entirely possible that he dreamed of one day having a position of authority.

---

256 Jeremiah 32:25 NASB

This distinction is important. Ambitions are very different from dreams. A dream springs out of something which God has planted in you, something that touches the core of who you are and what you are created to be. But a dream is also out of reach, when measured according to your own strength and abilities.

Ambition, on the other hand, is a bad thing.[257] The Greek word in the new testament for ambition (*eritheia*) can also be translated as selfishness or disputes. It is defined as "electioneering or intriguing for office."[258] In other words, an ambition is something that we desire to attain, and are willing to attain through our own efforts using the resources available to us. It is, in fact, the same attitude which led to the devil's fall.[259]

As servants of Jesus we must understand the difference between ambitions and dreams. Leaders who come into position through their own ambition will lead in a manner colored by ambition's ugliness. The tactics which they have used to attain their position will influence the manner in which they govern. And their fear that such tactics may be used against them will cause fear to spread through their regime.

> *Therefore if you have any encouragement from being united with Christ, if any comfort from his love, if any common sharing in the Spirit, if any tenderness and compassion, then make my joy complete by being like-minded, having the same love, being one in spirit and of one mind. Do nothing out of selfish ambition or vain conceit.*

---

257 See 2 Corinthians 12:20, Galatians 5:20, Philippians 2:3, James 3:14-16
258 Strongs lexicon, G2052
259 Isaiah 14:13-14

> *Rather, in humility value others above yourselves, not looking to your own interests but each of you to the interests of the others. In your relationships with one another, have the same mindset as Christ Jesus. (Philippians 2:1-5)*

When we are promoted to having greater authority in our community, it is *not* about control. It is all about blessing. In the Kingdom of Heaven, promotion is not given so that the person promoted can separate himself from the needs of the people around him. The greatest among you shall be the servant.[260]

True leadership is not about power, but about enabling. Many people expect leaders to lead by exercising power or manipulation. So when we come into positions of authority, they may fear how we might misuse our position. We must never succumb to this temptation. A true leader makes it possible for those around them to excel and even exceed the performance of their leader.[261]

How tragic it is, if removing oppression is the doorway that leads to promotion, and yet the authority gained thereby is used to control and manipulate. If a leader's understanding of freedom is implemented by force, the result is not blessing but something perverted. The Kingdom of Heaven is not established by force, by control, by trickery or by domination. The Kingdom of Heaven is a Kingdom of peace and blessing.

We must, at all costs, avoid the political spirit. In its simplest form, the political spirit says, "I oppose anything proposed by someone who is not on my side." In other words, the political spirit is not necessarily

---
[260] See Matthew 23:11, Mark 10:43-45
[261] See John 14:12

interested in solutions that will improve the situation at hand, but only in maintaining its own power. The political spirit demands loyalty, thrives on strife, and disregards truth. At its root you will find control, manipulation, oppression and self-righteousness.

For most of us, a promotion to take charge over our city will not manifest itself as a visible position of political leadership in our community. Though some Christians may be called to serve their communities through the political system, most of us will not walk through that doorway.

The Kingdom of Heaven resources at our disposal (a crown of beauty, the oil of gladness and a garment of praise) operate at an entirely different level. We are called to worship the Lord in the beauty of holiness.[262] Through a display of excellence, an attitude of thankfulness and joy, and an atmosphere of blessing and goodness we become pillars of stability and safety in whose presence people will find refuge. We will find that our counsel is heard, that our words carry an authority that leads people to listen intently. We will also find that our prayers carry weight, because our Lord also chooses to listen intently.

The restoration of cities is about bringing an end to oppression. Many throughout history[263] have been disturbed by injustice and tried to resolve it by creating a "just" system. But in the same manner as when Cain established the first city, any system established on the efforts of fallen humanity will fail to bring true justice.

---

262 Psalm 29:2, 96:9 KJV
263 among them Buddha, the prophet Muhammad and Karl Marx

The road to breaking the yoke of oppression passes through worship in the beauty of holiness. You become what you behold.[264] As we seek the face of our Lord in worship and prayer for blessing and favor upon our cities, the Kingdom of Heaven will come in ever greater measure.

> *But we urge you, brethren, to excel still more, and to make it your ambition to lead a quiet life and attend to your own business and work with your hands, just as we commanded you, so that you will behave properly toward outsiders and not be in any need. (1 Thessalonians 4:10b-12 NASB)*

Food for thought

Write down one or two of your dreams that involve promotion. How can you position your heart toward the fulfillment of those dreams?

---

264 1 John 3:2b

The Bride

Anticipation

Expectant anticipation can be one of the highest forms of adoration. Think, for example, of a young child in the weeks before Christmas. There is a tree in the living room, brightly decorated with enticing ornaments. And under the tree are colorful packages that are just screaming to be opened. This young child knows that under the tree are things which will bring her delight. But those things are off limits until Christmas day arrives. And the expectancy and anticipation of that moment generate excitement and enthusiasm which are dear to the hearts of the parents.

Quite similar for a bride is the time leading up to the wedding. The period of engagement is a time of great joy and preparation, a time buoyed by intimacy and unfettered emotions. Yet, there is a level of intimacy that is reserved for within the framework of marriage. And the anticipation of this joy makes the approach of the wedding both exciting and perhaps a bit frustrating.

> *At that time the Kingdom of Heaven will be like ten virgins who took their lamps and went out to meet the bridegroom. Five of them were foolish and five were wise. The foolish ones took their lamps but did not take any oil with them. The wise ones, however, took oil in jars along with their lamps. The bridegroom was a long time in coming, and they all became drowsy and fell asleep.*

> *At midnight the cry rang out: "Here's the bridegroom! Come out to meet him!" Then all the virgins woke up and trimmed their lamps.*
>
> *The foolish ones said to the wise, "Give us some of your oil; our lamps are going out."*
>
> *"No," they replied, "there may not be enough for both us and you. Instead, go to those who sell oil and buy some for yourselves."*
>
> *But while they were on their way to buy the oil, the bridegroom arrived. The virgins who were ready went in with him to the wedding banquet. And the door was shut. Later the others also came. "Lord, Lord," they said, "open the door for us!"*
>
> *But he replied, "Truly I tell you, I don't know you." Therefore keep watch, because you do not know the day or the hour. (Matthew 25:1-13)*

Jesus told this parable in the context of his return at the end of the age. And the key message is: Be always ready. But, we might ask, "Ready for what?"

In the case of this parable, the virgins were waiting for the bridegroom to arrive. The story implies that the role of these ten young ladies was to give the bridegroom an appropriate reception upon his arrival: To make him feel welcome, to illuminate his surroundings, and perhaps even to present him to the bride.

The bridegroom was a long time in coming. They knew that he would be coming, but they didn't know when. Clearly, they had to wait longer than they expected. And they fell asleep.

Falling asleep while they were waiting wasn't a problem in this story. There was nothing wrong with them having rested while they were waiting. That did not keep them from being ready to meet their calling when it came.

The real issue at hand was whether or not they had prepared themselves to meet the bridegroom in his time and in his way. Had they counted the cost? Had they laid a foundation that would stand in the face of unexpected difficulties or delays?

We do not know the day or the hour of Jesus' return. He is coming soon, and yet he is a long time in coming. We need to live as though he could come tomorrow or in a thousand years.

It is wrong to live our lives as though we will not live to see his return. With that line of thinking, it is easy to become self-centered and irresponsible. A bride who does not expect the bridegroom to come will not be focused on preparing herself for his arrival.

It is just as wrong to live our lives as though the future of this world does not matter. If you are convinced that his return is just around the corner, that you will soon be pulled into the sky and this world is going to burn; then you will not be a good steward in your own generation. And you certainly won't be motivated to invest into the generations that follow. This is where we find the foolish virgins. They were not prepared for the bridegroom to be a long time in coming. They figured that since he was coming soon, they didn't need to think about the long term.

The wise virgins, however, are an illustration of living in balance. They went out, expectantly looking for the bridegroom's impending arrival. But, since they had brought a supply of oil with them, they were also prepared for him to be a long time in coming. As the time passed, they carried on with their lives, filled with anticipation of the coming of the bridegroom and also equipped to meet him whenever he came.

The key to maintaining balance is a sense of childlike *expectancy*. Like the child who can hardly wait for Christmas to arrive, we are called to anticipate the return of the bridegroom with expectancy and joy. It is the anticipation that keeps us focused, however long we must wait.

And yet, anticipation is like the oil that could not be shared. You can't live for the long term on someone else's sense of expectancy. Before the bridegroom arrives, you must develop your own longing and your own desire. I can't get excited for you.

When the foolish virgins returned after having bought oil, they *expected* to be admitted to the wedding banquet. But they were refused entrance. Why? According to the bridegroom, it was because he did not know them. Perhaps they were mainly there because they wanted to eat and drink at the party.

The wise and foolish virgins point to the subtle but fundamental difference between expectation and expectancy.

The foolish virgins expected to have a place at the wedding banquet as a consequence of their position or actions. An expectation is a speculation about how or when or where something ought to happen. An expectation has an element of demand, and if not met brings an element of disappointment or anger.

Expectation is the spirit of entitlement's primary mode of operation.

Expectancy, on the other hand, is joy-based. The wise virgins were guided by their anticipation of the bridegroom's arrival. They didn't know when or how he would come, but they knew he would come and were joyfully content in that hope.

The difference between the wise and the foolish virgins went far deeper than whether or not they had a jar of oil in their hands. There was something about how the wise virgins prepared themselves for meeting the bridegroom that set them apart. The fact that they had oil with them was just a visible sign of something deep in their character. They weren't just looking for a happening, they were participants in a relationship.

I believe that the story of Esther becoming queen gives an insightful illustration of expectancy. After having been dishonored by his queen, King Xerxes had her deposed and then started a process to find a suitable replacement queen. It was a bit like a beauty pageant. A bunch of attractive young girls were gathered together and spent a year working on their outward beauty. Then, one by one, they went in to spend a night of intimacy with the king.

> And this is how she would go to the king: Anything she wanted was given her to take with her from the harem to the king's palace. In the evening she would go there and in the morning return to another part of the harem... She would not return to the king unless he was pleased with her and summoned her by name. When the turn came for Esther ... to go to the king, she asked for nothing

> *other than what Hegai, the king's eunuch who was in charge of the harem, suggested. And Esther won the favor of everyone who saw her. (Esther 2:13-15)*

I imagine that most of the girls in this competition very much wanted to be queen, while the part about being the king's spouse may not have been quite as appealing to them. So, when their time came and they took with them whatever they desired, their focus was probably on trying to spotlight themselves so that they would be chosen as queen. Most likely, these young virgins weren't exactly thrilled about having to spend the night in bed with this 40-something man whom they had never met. Their thoughts were probably more about getting through the night than about being together with the king. And yet they *expected* that with the right amount of self-promotion they could make enough of an impression to be chosen as queen.

Esther, however, appears to have gone into the situation with a perspective of *expectancy*. She chose only to take with her what the king's friend recommended, rather than trying to promote herself. And I imagine that with such an attitude, she was able to be *present* with the king during their time together. This could well be why the king saw something in her which he had not seen in any of the other girls. She wasn't just focused on becoming the queen. She let him get to know her.

Food for thought

What are you looking forward to as you wait for the return of the bridegroom? Escaping the tribulation? Getting accepted into the Kingdom? The punishment of the wicked? Or our union with the bridegroom?

*Are you expectantly awaiting the return of our Bridegroom?
Or are you waiting for him to meet your expectations?*

Transition

A wedding is a transition party. It is the event where two people who have found that they want to spend the rest of their lives together transition from being two individuals to becoming one family. Most newlyweds discover that life together is different from the life they lived as single. Transition is a time of change, but it is not a place to stay. The goal of this transition is to move into a joyful married life beyond the wedding day.

Before a wedding can take place, several things need to happen. First of all, the bride needs to be ready. We could also say that the bridegroom needs to be ready, but often he's been ready (or so he might think) since before he popped the question. Typically, what the bridegroom needs to do is show up at the right place and time. If the bridegroom arrives at the wedding before his bride is ready, he may be in for a long and frustrating wait. So it would make sense for the bridegroom to do everything within his power to insure that his bride will be equipped to make herself ready at the right time.

> *Now learn the parable from the fig tree: when its branch has already become tender and puts forth its leaves, you know that summer is near. Even so, you too, when you see these things happening, recognize [or know] that He [or it] is near, right at the door[s]. Truly I say to you, this generation [or race] will not pass away until all these things take place. Heaven and earth will pass away, but My words will not pass away. (Mark 13:28-31 NASB with footnotes)*

The key point of this parable is that there is a transition that will take place, and that we can recognize when the transition is about to take place.

When spring comes, I notice that leaves are budding on the trees. But seldom do I give much attention to the details of that budding process. I appreciate the return of bright green hillsides and look forward to the summer that is approaching. I am aware of the season and it does not take me by surprise. But I have only a limited interest in biology, so I am glad that I do not need to study the biology of the budding of leaves in order to enter into the summer. Rather, my time is often spent on being prepared for summer; be it things like stocking up on charcoal for the grill or preparing to paint the house or whatever.

In the same manner, I believe that (as in the parable) it will not be difficult for me to "see these things happening" and by them recognize the approach of the Bridegroom, provided that my focus is already on him and on that joyous life which marriage with him will bring.

Eschatology

Eschatology is the study of the end times, or more specifically it is an area of theology that is focused on the sequence of events leading up to the transition from the end of this age to the beginning of the next. To be honest, I am not very interested in eschatology – though I have been exposed to quite a bit of it.

Although many of Jesus' parables touch on various eschatological aspects, my primary goal is to look at how the parables of Jesus portray the King and his Kingdom. One thing which is clear is that the King and his Kingdom will continue from this age into the age to come. Although some may consider the events of the transition between the ages to be of great importance, I have a far greater interest in the nature of the King and the workings of his Kingdom than I have in the details of how the Kingdom will transition from the current age to the next one.

If you are looking for an in-depth discussion of how the parables of Jesus fit into the puzzle of what will happen in the end times, then this book may disappoint you in relation to that particular expectation. Even so, let me try to explain how I see things in a broader perspective.

Often, a focus on the details of the transition involves getting hung up on specific interpretations of unclear or symbolic passages of scripture. This often leads to fear, confusion and division – things which I prefer to avoid and which have no place in the culture of the Kingdom.

For example, in the parable of the weeds, at the end of the age the Son of Man will send his angels to weed out of his Kingdom everything that causes sin and everyone who does evil, and *then* the righteous will shine like the sun in the Kingdom. This order of events appears to be in conflict with other New Testament passages[265] describing an event (commonly called the "rapture") where all believers will be removed from this world prior to the judgment of those who do evil, and perhaps even before the end-times tribulations described in the book of Revelation.

---

265 Such as 1 Thessalonians 4:16-17, Revelation 11:12, and more

Trying to resolve this apparent inconsistency in scripture can easily lead to fear, confusion and division. But in my opinion, it is neither necessary nor important to resolve it at this time. So, what to do then? Rather than allowing doubt to arise in my heart because I am unable to wrap my mind around the enormous wisdom of God in this area, I choose instead to look intently to this unshakable King, secure in who he is.

> Then they gathered around him and asked him, "Lord, are you at this time going to restore the kingdom to Israel?" He said to them: "It is not for you to know the times or dates the Father has set by his own authority. But you will receive power when the Holy Spirit comes on you; and you will be my witnesses in Jerusalem, and in all Judea and Samaria, and to the ends of the Earth." (Acts 1:6-8)

These are the final words of Jesus before he was taken up into Heaven, so I believe they have substantial significance. My understanding of what Jesus is saying here is: Don't get all hung up in the details of the things that are to come, but rather stay focused on *being* the message of the Kingdom.

If you are looking for them, you will find plenty of believers who have focused on the details of the end of this age. They have their charts and their interpretations of the prophecies and various other hints in the Bible as to how the times and dates the Father has set by his own authority will work out.

But they don't all agree. Which is not surprising, since the Bible paints a picture that (at least on this topic) is shrouded in mystery. There are apparent contradictions, there is symbolism and there are hidden pieces of the puzzle. My understanding is that God has intentionally shrouded these things in mystery, because they are meant to be interpreted in light of the time to which they refer. As summer is approaching we will recognize the budding of the fig tree. Until that time, I am unsure how to interpret or resolve all of the parts of the puzzle. And the confident assertions of those who "are sure" do not make me any less unsure.

It was just the same at the time of Jesus' first coming. The Gospels describe clearly that there were Pharisees and teachers of the Law who, in their search for how and when the Messiah would come, knew the scriptures inside out. And yet, they totally missed it when Jesus walked among them. Why? Because in the pride and confidence of their understanding of the scriptures, they lost sight of their God.

But there were others, who didn't miss out. Simeon, who was waiting for the consolation of Israel and on whom the Spirit rested,[266] was one. Zacchaeus[267] was another. They were looking for the Lord and they recognized him when he came.

So I believe it will be at the end of the age. Those whose eyes and hearts are turned toward their Lord will recognize his approach and welcome him. But there is a risk that those who have a predetermined conviction of what, when and how the end of the age will look like, may (like the foolish virgins who lacked oil) be blinded by their convictions and miss it completely.

---

266 Luke 2:25-35
267 Luke 19:1-6

At the same time, I am *not* saying that we should ignore the issue of the end of this age. Revelation 1:3 states that there is a blessing on those who read, hear and take to heart the words of that prophecy. But *understanding* the prophecy is not listed there as a requirement for being blessed. I typically read the book of Revelation two or three times a year. It fascinates me, but there is plenty that I don't understand. And I don't let that bother me, because I believe that I will have the understanding I need when I need it for the events that will affect me – as long as my gaze is fixed on Jesus, who is the central focus of the revelation. This is faith and perseverance in practice.

For example, I recall the terrorist attack in 2001 on the World Trade Center in New York City. Time and time again, we saw on TV the video of the towers being hit by airplanes and then collapsing. And then I realized that I was experiencing something described in the book of Revelation: that people throughout the world would stand from afar, seeing "the smoke of her burning," and cry in anguish.[268] Now, I am not saying that the attack on the World Trade Center was the judgment of Babylon. But the mechanism of how the world responded is very much like what John saw in his prophecy.

I anticipate gaining more insight as we move closer to the end of the age. Things will take place which I will recognize as "this might well be that which was spoken of." But, in order to recognize things, we need to read and take to heart his words of prophecy with an open mind.

---

268 Revelation 18:9-19.

Just as in the day of Jesus: There are Old Testament prophecies which speak of the Messiah being the son of David, that he would be born of a virgin, that he would come from Bethlehem, that he would come from Egypt, that he would come from Galilee of the Gentiles. Taken at face value, there seems to be a lot of conflict between these prophecies. And that was one reason why the teachers of the Law rejected Jesus, the son of Joseph from Nazareth, since they couldn't see how he fit into the prophecies. And yet we know, after the fact, that Jesus did fulfill all of these seemingly conflicting words.

God in his wisdom has chosen to communicate prophecy in riddles.[269] But to Moses he spoke clearly and without riddles. Why? I believe it was because Moses was out to get a hold of God. He was not so interested in the how as in the who. And so he saw the form of the Lord.

A focus on trying to make sense of all the puzzle pieces will generate a certain degree of insecurity in us. A focus on the tribulations to come will perhaps instill fear in us (or at least in those around us). But a focus on our Lord and his faithfulness and goodness will keep us unshakable.

These things happening

Jesus told the parable of the budding fig tree after having been asked what would be the sign that the temple was about to be destroyed.[270] In response, Jesus listed a number of things that would happen, and then said that, like the budding fig tree, "When these things begin to

---

269 Numbers 12:6-8
270 Mark 13:2-4

take place, stand up and lift up your heads, because your redemption is drawing near."[271] These things that Jesus listed are:

- False messiahs
- Wars and rumors of wars
- Earthquakes and famines
- Persecution of believers, even to the dividing of families
- Abomination that causes desolation, destruction of Jerusalem
- Gospel of the Kingdom preached to all nations
- Sun and moon darkened, stars fall from the sky
- Son of Man coming in clouds

So, is the fig tree budding? I would say yes, but not fully so yet...

The first four points on this list have been happening more or less continuously throughout history. The abomination that causes desolation and the destruction of Jerusalem were carried out by the Romans in 70 AD (though these things could also be repeated at some future time). The gospel has not yet been preached to all people groups, though we may see that happen in our lifetimes. And the last two points have clearly not yet happened.

When we see the leaves budding on the trees, we know that summer is near. And summer is a good thing – a time of warmth and growth. But what is near when we see these things happening? Matthew and Mark say "it" (NIV) or "He" (NASB) is at the door. Luke says that the Kingdom of God is near. The context of this parable was the question: When will the temple be destroyed? Even

---

271 Luke 21:28

so, it is natural for us to connect "it" to the end of the age, the return of Jesus, the ushering in of his reign in the physical realm.

The transition from this age to the next encompasses a lot of upheaval. In particular, the prophecies of Daniel and John (in Revelation) point to turmoil and suffering way beyond our experience. But the transition ends with a wedding.

The leaves of a fig tree bud as the tree is moving into the season of bearing fruit. In the same manner, I look upon "these things happening" as steps toward the bride making herself ready so that her bridegroom can arrive at the right time.

Hastening his coming

> *The Lord is not slow about His promise, as some count slowness, but is patient toward you, not wishing for any to perish but for all to come to repentance. But the day of the Lord will come like a thief, in which the heavens will pass away with a roar and the elements will be destroyed with intense heat, and the earth and its works will be burned up. Since all these things are to be destroyed in this way, what sort of people ought you to be in holy conduct and godliness, looking for and hastening the coming of the day of God, because of which the heavens will be destroyed by burning, and the elements will melt with intense heat! (2 Peter 3:9-12 NASB)*

This passage contains an amazing instruction: to hasten the coming of the day of God. Think about it. Somehow or other we can influence the times and dates which the Father has set by his own authority. How can that be? What does it look like?

I believe that the key can be found earlier in the passage. The Lord does not wish for any to perish. To me this says that part of the bride making herself ready is for as many people as possible to come to repentance. When God created people, he blessed them and said that they were to be fruitful and increase in number. There is a blessing that follows population growth, because the heart of the Father is to see his Son joined to a worthy bride. Like the farmer in the parable of the weeds, he wants to see a maximum return from his field of wheat, and does not wish to see a single stalk fail to grow to its full potential.

Jesus said that one of these things that must happen before his return was that the gospel be preached to all nations. Paul has written that the god of this age has blinded the eyes of unbelievers so that they are unable to see the light of the gospel. And yet, the Lord is not slow about his return, but patient on account of his desire not only for the gospel to be preached but also lead to repentance. Hastening his coming involves acting to remove the blindness that keeps the nations from seeing the light of the gospel.

There are a few verses in the bible which tell that God hates wickedness. And we know that the wages of sin is death. Still, we don't see people being suddenly vaporized by a flash of lightning when they sin. Somehow, there appears to be a measure of sin that must be fulfilled[272] before God becomes compelled to pay out the wages of sin. The prayers that we pray contribute to

---

272 See Genesis 15:16 and Deuteronomy 9:4-5

tipping the balance against that destruction happening. There are bowls in heaven waiting to be filled with the fragrance of the bride's expressions of longing and adoration. When they are filled, the Lord moves and we can see cities and nations transformed. Could it be that the Lord awaits the time when all nations have had their gospel blindness healed?

The book of Revelation tells us that at the end of the age the glory and honor of the nations will be brought into the new Jerusalem.[273] If you think about it, that is a statement with huge implications. If we are expecting things to get worse, and lawlessness to increase, and evil to abound; then what is this glory and honor that the nations will carry so that the new Jerusalem can be made complete? If, at the end of the age, the nations are going to all stand in opposition to the Kingdom of Heaven, who will bring in the glory of these nations?

I believe that those who may look for judgments and tribulations as signs of the fig tree budding can be missing an important aspect of the heart of the Father. When I read through the prophets, especially Jeremiah and Ezekiel, there are tremendous judgments spoken. But it is also clear that these judgments are spoken from a heart whose longing is that the people would change so that God could rather relent and not bring judgment. That should also be the heart of his bride in our own day – a desire to influence our generation in such a way that the judgments prophesied for the end of the age would not come about.

It is not the will or desire of Father God that the nations of this world should end up under judgment. Prophecy is

---

273 Revelation 21:26

not fate. Or maybe it is – if we fail to intercede. Jonah prophesied judgment over Nineveh, but the Lord relented in the face of repentance. Jesus prophesied that Peter would deny him, but that was certainly not the Lord's will or his plan or his desire. It is true that our God is a Rock who does not change his mind. And yet, the Bible is full of examples where he *does* change his mind when his children ask him to show mercy rather than judgment. This illustrates just how much value he puts on our cry for mercy for the peoples.

The possibility exists for all nations to be found among the sheep, rather than among the goats. Our destiny as people of the faith of Abraham, that all of the world's people groups would be blessed through him, *can* become a reality. We really could see the Kingdom of God on Earth as it is in Heaven. It is not just an empty prayer.

Imagine how glorious the end of this age might be if we so influence our nations that God changes his mind about the judgments prophesied for the end of the age; just like when he changed his mind about the judgment that Jonah prophesied over Nineveh. He is, after all, the God who has no pleasure in the death of the wicked.[274]

Food for thought

Are you worried about how the end of the age will play out? How can looking toward the return of Jesus help you to draw closer to him as a friend? What steps to change the way you think should you take to bring your heart more in line with the Lord's heart, not wishing for any to perish?

---

274 Ezekiel 18:23, 32, 33:11

The Wedding

Most young girls dream of the day they will become a beautiful bride. The fairy tales found in so many cultures about some beautiful princess being courted (and perhaps rescued) by their prince charming are an indication that there is something planted in the heart of humanity which looks forward to a wedding.

And this should not be surprising. When God, after surveying all of the animals without finding a suitable companion for Adam, fashioned a mate out of the stuff of Adam's inner being,[275] it was a prophetic picture. For God the Father is looking to fashion a suitable bride for God the Son out of the stuff of his inner being (which is created in his own image).

> *The Kingdom of Heaven is like a king who prepared a wedding banquet for his son. He sent his servants to those who had been invited to the banquet to tell them to come, but they refused to come. Then he sent some more servants and said, "Tell those who have been invited that I have prepared my dinner: My oxen and fattened cattle have been butchered, and everything is ready. Come to the wedding banquet." But they paid no attention and went off—one to his field, another to his business. The rest seized his servants, mistreated them and killed them. The king was enraged. He sent his army and destroyed those murderers and burned their city. Then he said to*

---

275 Genesis 2:18-22

his servants, "The wedding banquet is ready, but those I invited did not deserve to come. So go to the street corners and invite to the banquet anyone you find." So the servants went out into the streets and gathered all the people they could find, the bad as well as the good, and the wedding hall was filled with guests. But when the king came in to see the guests, he noticed a man there who was not wearing wedding clothes. He asked, "How did you get in here without wedding clothes, friend?" The man was speechless. Then the king told the attendants, "Tie him hand and foot, and throw him outside, into the darkness, where there will be weeping and gnashing of teeth." For many are invited, but few are chosen. (Matthew 22:1-14) [See also Luke 14:16-24]

Outside

This parable touches on a number of things, so I will begin with what I consider to be the least pleasant aspect. Although it is clearly addressed by some of the parables we have already been through, such as the parable of the weeds and the parables of the minas/talents, I have put off addressing it until now.

The Kingdom of Heaven is very much about grace and restoration, but there is no getting around the fact that there will also be a judgment. This judgment is not inconsistent with the nature of the King or his Kingdom. We may not like it. We may think it unreasonable. But that will not change the King one bit.

Jesus used a number of phrases to describe a place of punishment, such as: "outside," "darkness," "blazing furnace," "where there will be weeping and gnashing of teeth" and "where the worms that eat them do not die, and the fire is not quenched." He referred to this place as "the eternal fire prepared for the devil and his angels" or "gehenna."[276] These descriptions paint a picture of a thoroughly unpleasant place, a place of irrevocable loss and torment, from which there is no escape. This punishment is primarily for the devil and his angels, but will also come upon those who choose to reject the wedding invitation.

In our day there is a debate as to whether or not this place is a reality or perhaps just a form of imagery. It is beyond the scope of this book to try to resolve that debate here. But we are looking at what the parables of Jesus tell us about the Kingdom of Heaven. And these parables point to dire consequences for those whom the King finds in opposition to him.

I see two distinct pathways that lead to being outside: There are those who refuse to accept the rule of the King. And there are those whose actions are inappropriate in the culture of the Kingdom.

In the parable of the weeds, Jesus explained that the weeds represent the people of the devil, who will be thrown into the fire at the end of the age. In the parable of the minas, upon his return the king commands that all who opposed his rule be slaughtered. So, too, in the parable of the dragnet.[277]

There are also examples of actions that are inappropriate in the culture of the Kingdom. In the parable of the talents, the servant who buried his talent was thrown

---

276 Often translated as "hell."
277 Matthew 13:47-50

outside. The same was true for the servant who was unfaithful during his master's absence[278] and for those who did not do "for the least of these" in the parable of the sheep and the goats.

Note that Jesus is quite matter of fact about the subject. He does not skirt the issue. Neither does he use this possibility of being put outside to frighten or manipulate his listeners. He simply states that the consequences will come into play at the end of the age. When that time comes, those who have not accepted his rule and those who are not in the habit of behaving appropriately in the culture of his Kingdom will find themselves left outside.

In the case of the wedding, those guests who were originally invited did not accept the invitation. In fact, many went into opposition, beating and murdering the king's messengers in a manner reminiscent of the parable of the tenants. As a result, the king destroyed them.

There was also a guest who was found not wearing wedding clothes. He had been invited to the wedding feast, but he dishonored both his host and the other guests by not clothing himself appropriately for the event.

Perhaps he was dressed in filthy clothes, which symbolize sin.[279] He should rather have taken the time to clothe himself in a manner that would bring honor to the king who had invited him. In the New Testament, this is described as putting on Christ.[280] When Paul wrote that

---

278 Matthew 24:42-51
279 See Isaiah 64:6, Zechariah 3:3-4, Revelation 3:4
280 See Romans 13:14, Galatians 3:27, Colossians 3:12, Revelation 3:18, 19:8

he himself no longer lived, but rather Christ lived in him, he was writing about clothing himself in the nature, character and behavior of Jesus Christ his Lord.

It could, however, be that the guest was overdressed. A wedding is primarily about the bride and groom. It is a mistake to go to a wedding dressed in a manner which steals attention from the bride or groom. This is pride,[281] which is highly offensive in the culture of the Kingdom.

Either way, once this man accepted the invitation to attend the wedding feast, he also became responsible for clothing himself properly. I do not believe that his lack of wedding clothes was an economic issue. Luke's version of the parable clearly states that the poor and disabled were invited (or perhaps compelled) to come. So the king was well aware of their own inability to clothe themselves. Rather, they would have been provided with appropriate clothes on their way to the banquet and needed only to put on that clothing. Choosing to wear your own clothing rather than that which the king has given you for the occasion will certainly not bring honor to the king.

Although the parables of Jesus make a strong case for the reality of hell, they are not meant to create fear. We are *invited* to a feast, and a feast is a good thing. We are called to be clothed appropriately, but we are given the clothing and need only to put it on.

You may be wondering what kind of clothes our King provides. The third chapter of the letter to the Colossians speaks of putting aside (or taking off or putting to death) things which are inappropriate in the Kingdom of God, and then putting on (or clothing yourself in) things more appropriate. These things are not rules to be followed,

---

281 See Psalm 73:6, 1 Peter 5:5

but rather a process of clothing yourself in royal robes. When Israel said to Moses that they wanted him to talk to God and then tell them what to do,[282] they chose to reject royal robes. The result was an insurmountable set of rules to follow, because they chose servanthood over relationship. The servant does not have an inheritance in the king, but the invited wedding guest may be clothed with dignity and honor.

The bride

> Let us rejoice and be glad and give him glory! For the wedding of the Lamb has come, and his bride has made herself ready. Fine linen, bright and clean, was given her to wear." (Fine linen stands for the righteous acts of God's holy people.) Then the angel said to me, "Write this: Blessed are those who are invited to the wedding supper of the Lamb!" And he added, "These are the true words of God." (Revelation 19:7-9)

What do you picture when you think of a bride who has made herself ready? It is not uncommon for a bride to spend months preparing for her wedding day. There is the wedding dress and the flowers and the hairdo and more. When the wedding day finally does arrive and she makes her entrance in stunning beauty, her groom knows that it has been worth the wait.

God the Father has been preparing a bride for his Son from the foundation of the world. Since before the creation of mankind, God the Father has been shaping a body of believers to be a suitable partner for God the Son.

---

282 Exodus 20:18-19

Jesus will have only one bride. This suitable partner is not you or me but all believers functioning together in unity of beauty and purpose. I can hardly grasp what that may look like. It boggles my mind. Considering how challenging it is for a family or small fellowship to live and walk together in unity, I am at times overwhelmed by the huge disparity between where we, the Church, are today and where we are called to be. But, there will come a day when there will be a wedding and the bride will be ready.

Peter encouraged us to speed the coming of "the day of God."[283] For years, I have understood that to mean that we must preach the gospel to the entire world so that the end would come.[284] But, that is only one side of the coin. Another issue is the bride having made herself ready.

What does that look like? Words like pure, spotless, holy, blameless and righteous come to mind. Paul wrote of jealously working to present us as a pure virgin to one husband, Christ.[285] He also wrote about Christ washing his bride with water through the Word.[286] These things speak to our sanctification, both as individual believers and as a body of believers. This sanctification is not something we must accomplish in order to become acceptable to the Bridegroom. And yet, it is very much a part of the bride making herself ready. The cleansing which makes us acceptable took place on the Cross. But the beautification that makes us *ready* is a process which continues to this day. We need to choose purity, we need

---

[283] 2 Peter 3:11-14
[284] An interpretation of Matthew 24:14
[285] 2 Corinthians 11:2
[286] Ephesians 5:25-27

to allow ourselves to be washed, we need to do the righteous acts that have been prepared for us.

The bride is also described as a city,[287] beautifully adorned with jewels. And her measurements: as wide and high as she is long. Although I don't quite grasp why that is beautiful, the context of the passage leads me to believe that it certainly is. Perhaps this unity of measurement is a reflection of the unity of an uncountable number of the children of God moving, living and breathing as *one* bride. If so, then speeding the coming of the day of God also involves learning, even now, to live in unity as the people of Christ. I do not believe that unity in this sense is to be achieved through organizational structures or through conformity of understanding. Rather, I believe that we are called to move into oneness of heart.

Our only true model of oneness of heart is found in the relationship between God the Father, God the Son and God the Holy Spirit. It stands to reason, then, that by fixing our gaze on Jesus and learning of his ways, their practice of oneness will rub off on us. And the more we do it together with believers with whom we don't necessarily feel comfortable (to start with), the more we will grow in unity.

So, at the least, a bride who has made herself ready is beautifully adorned, with dignity and purpose, whose gaze is fixed on her beloved.

I once had a colleague who had a humorous placard on the wall in her workspace. Under the subject "How to impress a woman" it listed at least 20 things like romancing her, honoring her, complimenting her, etc.

---

287 Revelation 21:2-3, 9-16

The second part was much simpler. (This is rather blunt, but please don't get offended.) "How to impress a man: Show up naked; bring food."

Now, there is an element of truth here. A bride who has prepared herself is able and willing to let her beloved see who she really is, without any pretense or covering, without inhibitions or fear. If we are the bride of Christ and we want to impress our beloved, then there is nothing to be gained by trying to cover over who we are with some kind fancy, but misleading, apparel. After all, he has x-ray vision, so it won't fool him anyhow. But when we come to him in all our naked honesty, he responds with intimacy.

And then there is the food part. Of course, it is only natural that a wedding includes a feast.

The feast

Let him lead me to the banquet hall, and let his banner over me be love. (Song of Songs 2:4)

Have you noticed that much of Old Testament worship took place in a context of feasting? Through the course of the year, a number of feasts were prescribed in the Mosaic Law. Several of these were pilgrimage feasts, where the believers traveled to the tabernacle or temple so they could celebrate together as one people.

One of the major activities going on at these feasts was sacrifices and offerings. Now some of the sacrifices were wholly given over to God, but in many cases the meat of the sacrifice was returned to the worshiper[288] to be eaten together with his household.

When you sacrifice an entire sheep or goat or ox, there is a lot of meat. The rules of the day basically required that all of the meat be eaten there and then. In order to get that to work, it was normal to make it a party. Invite all of the neighbors and friends. Let there be no waste.

In this kind of a culture, even the poor and homeless would not need to go hungry. In a community of any size, there would always be someone who needed help getting their sacrifice eaten. The result is a culture where worship, feasting, joy and care for the needy all flow together in a natural way. In fact, the instructions for the tithe pointed to this party atmosphere:

> *Be sure to set aside a tenth of all that your fields produce each year. Eat the tithe of your grain, new wine and olive oil, and the firstborn of your herds and flocks in the presence of the LORD your God at the place he will choose as a dwelling for his Name, so that you may learn to revere the LORD your God always. But if that place is too distant and you have been blessed by the LORD your God and cannot carry your tithe (because the place where the LORD will choose to put his Name is so far away), then exchange your tithe for silver, and take the silver with you and go to the place the LORD your God will choose. Use the silver to buy whatever you like: cattle, sheep, wine or other fermented drink, or anything you wish. Then you and your household shall eat there in the presence of the LORD your God and rejoice. And do not*

---

288 Though often the priests and/or Levites were given a portion.

> neglect the Levites living in your towns, for they have no allotment or inheritance of their own. At the end of every three years, bring all the tithes of that year's produce and store it in your towns, so that the Levites (who have no allotment or inheritance of their own) and the foreigners, the fatherless and the widows who live in your towns may come and eat and be satisfied, and so that the LORD your God may bless you in all the work of your hands. (Deuteronomy 14:22-29)

Even in the weekly sabbath celebration, food had a central place. Among other things, the sabbath was an opportunity for the family to gather at mealtimes and talk about the goodness of the Lord in a context of daily life and fellowship. Parents do not normally use the model of classroom instruction and lectures to teach their children how to live. Rather, most of what a child learns while growing up is learned from observing the lives of their parents. And in a healthy setting, a lot of the wisdom of life is learned around the dinner table.

We see this also in the life of Jesus. Although he did sometimes teach publicly, in the synagogue or temple, in the fields and on the seashore, it was those who followed him in the daily activities of life that were discipled. Mealtimes were undoubtedly a frequent setting where Jesus and his followers talked and shared and laughed together in a way that taught them more about who Jesus and his Father are than any of his preaching would have done.

In the parable of the wedding banquet, after the guests who were initially invited rejected their invitation, the king acted in a way that reflects wisdom:

> *Lady Wisdom has built and furnished her home; it's supported by seven hewn timbers. The banquet meal is ready to be served: lamb roasted, wine poured out, table set with silver and flowers. Having dismissed her serving maids, Lady Wisdom goes to town, stands in a prominent place, and invites everyone within sound of her voice: "Are you confused about life, don't know what's going on? Come with me, oh come, have dinner with me! I've prepared a wonderful spread—fresh-baked bread, roast lamb, carefully selected wines. Leave your impoverished confusion and live! Walk up the street to a life with meaning." (Proverbs 9:1-6 The Message)*

The imagery here portrays a close relationship between participating in a banquet and gaining wisdom. And the process of gaining wisdom is all about relationship. Wisdom is not information or knowledge, but it is experience gained through fellowship. And one of the best venues for that kind of fellowship is around the banqueting table.

Being known

> *Your oils have a pleasing fragrance, Your name is like purified oil; Therefore the maidens love you. (Song of Songs 1:3 NASB)*

A wedding banquet is primarily about fellowship. Yes, it is a party, but a party with no guests does not fulfill its potential. That is why it was important to the king for his banquet hall to be filled with guests. He wants to relate to as many guests as possible. The Kingdom of Heaven is like a banquet hall that is meant to be filled with guests.

So, although the parable of the wedding banquet touches on the fact that those who reject the invitation will be left outside, the parable is not so much about the possibility of not being included as about the goodness of God wooing. From before the beginning of time, God the Father has been preparing a bride for his Son and a daughter-in-law for himself. It is a goal that is dear to his heart. He is not trying to put as many outside as possible. His desire is for the banquet hall to be filled with guests.

However, there is an issue that arises frequently when Jesus touches on the fact that there are some who will be left outside. He says: "I don't know you."[289] We often tend to have a focus on getting to know God. But how good are we at letting him get to know us?

How do you feel about laying bare your weaknesses and failures to God our Father? What about your dreams and secret desires? Perhaps you find it easier to relate to Jesus and you are more able to open up your heart to him. Still, our Father is inviting you to the banquet, desiring to share good food and wine with you in joyous fellowship.

One evening, our daughter's boyfriend of a few months sent me a message asking if he could come by and talk to us. My first thought was, "Hmm, it seems a bit soon for him to be coming to ask for our daughter's hand in marriage..."[290] We agreed on an evening that he would come visit. When he came, it turned out that it wasn't so he could ask "the question." Rather, his purpose took us

---

289 Matthew 7:23, 25:12, Luke 13:25-27
290 Though I do not believe that a young man *must* ask permission of their prospective father-in-law, it is certainly a good way to honor the father of your beloved and build a good foundation for a long-lasting relationship with him.

by surprise: Since he was serious about his growing relationship with our daughter, he wanted to take time and get to know us parents, without our daughter being present. That made an impression on me!

We are not only invited into a marriage relationship with the Son, but also into a child relationship with the Father. Without developing both relationships, we fall short of our calling.

> *For in Him the whole fullness of Deity (the Godhead) continues to dwell in bodily form [giving complete expression of the divine nature]. And you are in Him, made full and having come to fullness of life [in Christ you too are filled with the Godhead-Father, Son and Holy Spirit-and reach full spiritual stature]. And He is the Head of all rule and authority [of every angelic principality and power]. (Colossians 2:9-10 Amplified)*

Now, I am not saying that you should try to dissect all of this in order to have the right relationship to each of the distinct persons in the Godhead. It doesn't have to be that complex. It is so much easier to just let yourself be wrapped up in the embrace of a lover and the embrace of a father. Be made full and experience the fullness. It has always been his longing to be with us, and in us. "And the two will become one."

This is where what I consider to be perhaps the most fulfilling moment of all history takes place. When the voice of the Father, shouting excitedly from his throne, says: "Look! God's dwelling place is now among the people!"[291]

---

291 Revelation 21:3

Making Herself Ready

We know that when Christ appears, we shall be like him, for we shall see him as he is. (1 John 3:2b)

It is perhaps most common to think of this truth as referring to the time of the return of Jesus. And there is no doubt that is the main thrust. And yet, I believe that the principle applies in our daily lives as well – the more we fix our gaze on Jesus and gain insight into who he really is, the more we will become like him. And the more like him we become, the more we will move toward becoming a bride who has made herself ready.

When I was a child, a shift began to take place in the culture in which I grew up. There were some good reasons for some of the changes that took place, but in retrospect I believe that the changes came about mostly as part of a strategy laid down by the enemy of our souls long before I was born. This shift was that my culture began to move away from it being common for a child to grow up in a family together with their mother and father and siblings.

Today, in most western societies, it is not uncommon for a child to grow up without living with, or perhaps even knowing, their father and grandfathers. This has lead to a generation of young people without good role models for what a father can be. Which, in turn, has greatly hindered many people's ability to see God as a Good Father. Much of the first part of this book touches on this issue.

In recent years, another shift has been taking place. Again, some of the specific societal changes brought about by this shift appear to be good things. After all, neither inequality nor discrimination are things that we should accept in society. And yet, there is a pattern to this shift which leads me to believe that once again we are seeing the fruit of the enemy's strategy.

This time around, the shift has to do with gender identity. Things which, in my youth, would hardly have been thinkable are now becoming front page political issues. It is a cultural disruption which is re-definng marriage and family, and even gender, away from that which has been accepted as fact in pretty much all cultures through pretty much all of history. In the past few years, most western nations have changed their laws from a position of defining marriage as the lifelong union of one man and one woman, to something more fluid and flexible. And from there, questions are being raised as to how, when or where to define a person's gender.

I do not believe that these things are happening accidentally or randomly. I believe that the societal shift away from the normality of a father, mother and siblings family unit is the result of the enemy's strategy to discredit and destroy common understanding of what a father is, in order to confuse people and drive them away from Father God. In the same manner, I believe that the more recent societal shift which is re-defining marriage and gender is the result of the enemy's strategy to discredit and destroy what wedding and marriage are, in order confuse people and drive them away from God the Son, our coming Bridegroom.

Now, I do not believe that the strategies of the enemy have taken God by surprise. And like the unshakable farmer, God is not likely to let these petty attacks of the enemy dictate his purposes.

In recent years, we have seen a revelation of God as a Good Father increasing in much of the Church. And it may well be that we are on the verge of seeing a new revelation of what it means for the Church to be a beautiful bride. The Father is preparing a bride for his Son, and that bride is making herself ready.

> *Now no one after lighting a lamp covers it over with a container, or puts it under a bed; but he puts it on a lampstand, so that those who come in may see the light. For nothing is hidden that will not become evident, nor anything secret that will not be known and come to light. So take care how you listen; for whoever has, to him more shall be given; and whoever does not have, even what he thinks he has shall be taken away from him. (Luke 8:16-18 NASB)*

In the midst of society's gender confusion, it is the Lord's desire that a pure and spotless bride would shine forth. In a time such as this, he calls his bride to make herself ready in the beauty of holiness. The lies and distortions brought about by the strategy of the enemy will wither and fade in the light of the beauty of a bride who has made herself ready.

With that in view, what follows is a summary of principles of the Kingdom of Heaven, as covered in this book. My prayer is that they will help us to more clearly see Jesus as he is, and thereby help to increase his reflection in his bride.

As you read these principles, please don't read them as a list of rules or instructions that you must follow. Look at them rather as beautiful garments, the adornment of a bride to be. It's all about a Father providing for his children and a Bridegroom preparing a place for his bride.

- **Belonging**: God has always been our Father and we have always belonged to him and belonged in his Kingdom. His passion is to see our hearts restored to him ever more fully.

- **Celebration**: Celebration is the natural response of Kingdom inhabitants, especially whenever someone is restored to where they belong.

- **Grace**: A core value, or perhaps *the* core value, of the Kingdom is grace. Grace is the fragrance that is released when the righteousness of God is enveloped by the love of God.

- **Honor**: In the Kingdom of Heaven, everyone is to be treated with honor. Not only parents, those who have gone before us, and those who hold positions of leadership; but even those with whom we disagree and those whom we consider to be rule-breakers.

- **Speech**: When speaking to or about others, our speech should reflect the culture of the Kingdom. Especially those whose actions are not honorable should experience from children of the King speech that is seasoned with grace and honor.

- **Father**: The King in this Kingdom is not a judge, but a father. And perhaps the most important discovery to be made in the Kingdom is that this is a good thing. Being a son or daughter to the Father is the core of your calling and destiny.

- **Sons and daughters**: All of the people in the Kingdom of Heaven are sons or daughters. None of us are called to be servants. Even though serving this King is not a bad thing, it is less than he has called us to. He wants to know and be known by his children.

- **Holiness**: In the Kingdom of Heaven, holiness is a result of walking in step with the King. Following the rules without following the Ruler will lead to self-righteousness without leading to holiness.

- **Home**: The Kingdom of Heaven is our true home. It is where we were created to live. It is what we are made for. And more than anything else, what makes it home is being there with the Father.

- **Fairness**: The King is always fair, and he treats all of his children in a *fair* manner. But he does not treat them all in the *same* manner, because each of us is unique. In the Kingdom of Heaven, comparing your circumstances with those of another person is actually a very ugly thing, because it implies that the King is unfair.

- **Extravagance**: The Kingdom of Heaven has boundless resources, and the King is extravagant in making them available. But he is not wasteful. His gifts are given freely wherever there is a potential that they will be received.

- **Communication**: In the Kingdom of Heaven, the basis for communication is friendship. Friends communicate by sharing their hearts with one another rather than giving instructions to each other.

- **Thorns**: Worry, fear, and lack of trust are thorns that will strangle the life of the believer. They are in opposition to the King and his Kingdom. The antidote is thankfulness and generosity.

- **Steadfastness**: The Kingdom of Heaven rests on a sure foundation, allowing us to confidently say: "I refuse to let the actions of the enemy dictate the course of my life." The enemy of the Kingdom has been disarmed, so there is nothing to fear and no reason to mount a counter-attack.

- **Punishment**: The King does not need to punish those who sin against him in order to maintain his security or his majesty. It is his nature to view every situation from a perspective of grace.

- **Potential**: The King views us in light of our potential rather than our performance. When faced with lack of fruit, he provides what is needed to bring forth fruit.

- **Power**: In the Kingdom of Heaven, true power is demonstrated through weakness and true victory is achieved through apparent loss. Setting out to gain victory through strength, power, or dominion is not the Kingdom approach.

- **Standing firm**: Victory in the Kingdom is not won by attacking the enemy, but by standing firm and resisting his attacks. His strength lies in deceiving us to come against him in strength. Those who stand firm in their submission to and dependence on the King will see the strength of the enemy evaporate.

- **Mercy**: Judgment in the Kingdom of Heaven is exercised from the seat of mercy. And the law in force is a law of freedom. Mercy triumphs over judgment.
- **Freedom**: Freedom is not doing whatever you want, or deciding what happens in your life. In fact, wanting or needing to direct the circumstances of your own life is actually a sign of bondage to fear and/or to an orphan spirit. True freedom is being so secure in the King and the culture of his Kingdom that you naturally choose to honor others, even though it may cost you something.
- **Insignificance**: In the economy of Heaven, it is often the insignificant things which have true value. And those things which we may consider to be significant often have little or no value in the Kingdom.
- **Rights**: As sons and daughters of the King, we are royalty. This gives us the privilege of laying down our rights in the face of the needs or misdeeds of others.
- **Humility**: Humility is having such confidence in the King that you completely trust him with your life; and having such security in your position and value as a child of the King that you don't need to demonstrate it to anyone else.
- **Passion**: Passion is highly valued in the culture of the Kingdom. Passion is both a consequence and a

catalyst of our faith. Where passion is lacking, it will often be substituted with legalism.

- **Granting freedom**: Forgiveness is granting freedom by canceling debts (both economic and otherwise). The culture of the Kingdom of Heaven is violated whenever we would insist on restitution rather than setting the debtor free.

- **Forgiveness**: Forgiveness is releasing the offender from the demands of the accuser. It is abandoning any claim to recompense or punishment. It releases freedom, both to the offender and to the offended.

- **Blessing**: The currency of the culture of freedom is blessing. Blessings wither if they are not passed on. Curses wither in the presence of blessings.

- **Reconciliation**: It is the King's desire that every one of his sons and daughters should be walking under the cover of his safety. When an offense has occurred, the keys to that safe place are our choice to forgive and restore.

- **Value**: The redemption which Jesus purchased for us is freely given to us. While, at the same time, walking fully in the Kingdom of God costs everything. Our hearts follow after what we value, and what we value tends to follow the price we have paid.

- **Presence**: The presence of the King is both terrifying and inviting, both dangerous and secure, both overwhelming and comforting. It is the *one thing* worth everything.

- **Repentance**: To repent is to change the way you think. The Kingdom of Heaven is so different from the ways of this world that you need to change the way you think in pretty much every area of life. But the degree to which we are able to change is related to our willingness to trust and submit to the King and his unfamiliar ways.

- **Fruit**: Fruitfulness in the Kingdom of Heaven comes from bringing pleasure to the King. He is not interested in ritual practice, but he longs for relationship with his children.

- **Fellowship**: Much of what happens in the Kingdom is uneventful. To a great degree, Kingdom life is the family spending time together.

- **Healing**: In the fulness of the Kingdom there is no sickness, no injury, no captivity, no bondage and no death. Our calling is not to hold out until we come into that fulness, but to see these aspects of the Kingdom grow around us in our daily lives. Our calling is to be distributors of redemption, healing and deliverance.

- **Freedom of choice**: In the Kingdom of Heaven, making right choices only has value when there is also the freedom to choose wrongly. Where there is no choice there is no room for true love to develop.

- **Structure**: Structures have no value in and of themselves in the Kingdom of Heaven. Rather, structures exist to facilitate strengthening and deepening the relationships between the Father and his children. The goal is bringing pleasure to the King and preparing a bride for her Bridegroom.

- **Influence**: Our calling as citizens of the Kingdom is to work through the culture in which we are placed, so that it is lifted up and improved, just as yeast causes bread to rise. We are not called to take control, but rather to bless and serve those who are leaders in the culture.

- **Creativity**: The King makes his resources available to us for the purpose of bringing his Kingdom near. But rather than micromanaging, he releases us to further the interests of his Kingdom by using our creativity and giftings in an atmosphere of freedom.

- **Wealth**: In the Kingdom of Heaven, the purpose of wealth is to spread blessing. Wealth is to be held lightly so that it can easily be poured out to bless others. Those who are faithful to generate blessing with little will be entrusted with much.

- **Excellence**: The Kingdom of Heaven is a kingdom of excellence. Excellence multiplies the value and effect of the things we do. And it terrifies the enemies of the Kingdom.

- **Restoration**: Restoration is a high priority in the Kingdom of Heaven. The King's desire is for the chaos and lawlessness of our world to be replaced by the peace, rest and freedom of the Kingdom.

- **Anticipation**: The joyful expectation of things to come carries a high value in the Kingdom of Heaven. Our anticipation of these things will be reflected in how we prepare ourselves for them.

Faithfulness looks to the goal regardless of how far off it may be.

- **Mystery**: The King shares his plans for the future of his Kingdom with his friends in a manner that is shrouded in mystery. For his friends, who trust him completely, this is not a problem. A need to have a sense of control over the events of the future is a symptom of a person who struggles with trusting the King.

- **Outside**: There is a place outside of the Kingdom. Those who oppose the rule of the King and those who are unwilling to live according to the culture of the Kingdom will find themselves left outside.

- **Unity**: The Son of the King is looking forward to a bride that has made herself ready. There will be only one bride. Among other things, making herself ready means that the company of believers will learn to walk together in oneness of heart and purpose.

- **Party**: The Kingdom of Heaven is a party! All of creation is looking forward to that time when the bride makes her stunning appearance and sits down together with her Bridegroom at the table of fellowship and feasting.

Twice in the Apostle John's vision of heaven he heard the worshipers there cry out about this bride making herself ready:

> *And they sang a new song, saying: "You are worthy to take the scroll and to open its seals, because you were slain, and with your blood you purchased for God persons from every tribe and*

> *language and people and nation. You have made them to be a kingdom and priests to serve our God, and they will reign on the earth." (Revelation 5:9-10)*

> *"Let us rejoice and be glad and give him glory! For the wedding of the Lamb has come, and his bride has made herself ready. Fine linen, bright and clean, was given her to wear." (Fine linen stands for the righteous acts of God's holy people.) (Revelation 19:7-8)*

The Lamb that was slain has purchased a people and made them into a kingdom. And the bride has made herself ready by clothing herself in righteous acts that were given to her. There are two sides to the coin here: The Lamb has made them into a kingdom, and she has made herself ready. The Lamb who was slain is renewing and transforming our minds in accordance with the culture of his Kingdom. At the same time, it is the bride who is clothing herself in these righteous acts he has given us to wear.

The forty-plus items in the list above are like fine linen. They are beautiful garments that have been chosen for us to enhance our loveliness. They are not meant to be left in a heap in the corner. Rather, they are made to be worn in a combination of stunning beauty and pleasing comfort. They have been designed and fashioned specifically to fit us well.

> *"For we are His workmanship, created in Christ Jesus for good works, which God prepared beforehand so that we would walk in them." (Ephesians 2:10 NASB)*

Now this two-sided coin could trick us into forgetting our role in the dance. Although it is the bride's responsibility to clothe herself, it is not her responsibility to make or even acquire the clothes. They have been given to her. The fine linen, the good works, are *his* workmanship, prepared by *him*. We need only to walk clothed in beauty. I think this is what Jesus was describing in the parable of the growing seed:

> *He also said, "This is what the kingdom of God is like. A man scatters seed on the ground. Night and day, whether he sleeps or gets up, the seed sprouts and grows, though he does not know how. All by itself the soil produces grain – first the stalk, then the head, then the full kernel in the head. As soon as the grain is ripe, he puts the sickle to it, because the harvest has come." (Mark 4:26-29)*

As we wander into the culture of the Kingdom, embracing the love of our Father the King and of our coming Bridegroom, the seeds of that culture grow and become mature and fruitful. The bride makes herself ready by walking in that love.

God is love. He is without sin. In him there is no spot or wrinkle. As we allow his love to fill our hearts, there will be less and less room for sin there. The love of God poured into our hearts[292] washes us clean and transforms our minds. As his love fills us, we are transformed into the beauty of holiness. And once the bride has been made ready, the wedding feast will commence.

At the end of the passover supper, before Jesus was arrested in the garden, he said some passionate things to his Father:

---

292 Romans 5:5

> *Now this is eternal life: that they know you, the only true God, and Jesus Christ, whom you have sent. I have brought you glory on earth by finishing the work you gave me to do. And now, Father, glorify me in your presence with the glory I had with you before the world began. I have revealed you to those whom you gave me out of the world. (John 17:3-6a)*

First, Jesus says that those who know the King and the Bridegroom have eternal life. True life is in knowing our God.

Second, he says that he has finished the work he was given to do. Interestingly, Jesus says this *before* he has died on the cross. So what was the work he had finished? It looks like he answers that question by saying, "Father, I have revealed you to them."

It is the revelation of God as a Father that changes us. This King, this Holy God Almighty, this Consuming Fire is revealed to be a God of Love. As we dance the dance of love with Father, Son and Holy Spirit, their love clothes us with the beauty of holiness.[293]

The Father has prepared a wedding for his Son. Both Father and Son are looking forward, with great anticipation and great joy, to that wedding day. They are awaiting a bride: The church in this world. And they are nurturing and providing for her during her time of preparation[294] in this world. But, the wedding day is *not* the goal. They are waiting for a bride who has made herself ready to *live* in the Kingdom of Heaven. They are waiting for a bride who belongs in their presence, who

---

293 See Psalm 96:9
294 See Esther 2:12

feels at home in their culture, and whose beauty makes them say, "Wow!"

Index of Parables

The wise and foolish builders 10
The lost coin 23
The prodigal son 26
The sower 63
The weeds 80
The barren fig tree 91
The seed that dies 96
Positions at a feast 113
The two debtors 118
The workers in the vineyard 121
The unforgiving servant 130
The lost sheep 142
The hidden treasure 149
The pearl of great price 149
Counting the cost 159
The two sons 161
The wicked farmers 164
The mustard seed 199
The yeast 199
The sheep and the goats 203
The minas 206
The dishonest manager 214
The master and servant 222
The ten virgins 240
The budding fig tree 247
The great banquet 259
A lamp under cover 276
The growing seed 286

Acknowledgments

I am thankful ...

Mostly, I am thankful for the freedom that Papa God has poured out over me; and the increasing experience of that freedom as I walk deeper into the revelation of who Papa is. I am thankful to be part of a loving family and fellowship of believers. Their support and friendship through the months spent preparing this book has been a real blessing.

Although the words of this book are my own, I am indebted to many for introducing me to the concepts herein. Trevor Galpin has helped me to see the Father more clearly throughout the gospels. I highly recommend his book, "Jesus and His Father by his family and friends." My understanding of sonship has been greatly influenced by the teaching of Fatherheart Ministries and the teaching of Arthur Burk. Arthur is also the source of the number line concept in *The Business of the Kingdom*. Pelle Karlsson's book "Korsets princip" (which sadly has not been translated to English, as far as I know) has laid much of the foundation for my understanding of the material in the chapter *To Lose is to Win*. The concept of excellence as a tool for dispersing oppression is based on Eric Johnson's interpretation of Zechariah's vision. Many of the concepts in *The Business of the Kingdom* build upon the teaching of Ed Silvoso, Bill Johnson and Kris Vallotton. And several of the insights in the chapter *The Prodigal Son's Father* were first shown to me by my wise and perceptive wife, Ellen.

Ingrid, my daughter. Thank you for your beautiful cover artwork. I am so often amazed by what you see and then commit to canvas.

A special thanks to Arthur Burk, Christine Clifton-Thornton, Sindre Grov, Esther Kienast, Øyvind Knudsen, Alejandro Serrano, John R. Snider and Christoffer Thimfors, whose valuable input has helped me to sharpen the focus of the book.

About the author

Bruce McKibben has lived in the city of Bergen since he came to Norway from Alaska in 1990. He is married, has three children and one grandchild (so far). He is employed in the electronics industry, is a leader in a house church in downtown Bergen, and has a heart for the church in the city. This is his second book. He can be reached at vandre@barbeint.no

Also by Bruce McKibben

Å vandre Hans veier, 2014, utgitt av Gjenreising Norsk Forlag, www.frihet.no

Walking His Ways, 2014, rewritten from the original Norwegian, available on Kindle